# Leo Sowerby

# AMERICAN

*Composers*

For a list of books in the series, please see our
website at www.press.uillinois.edu.

# Leo Sowerby

*Joseph Sargent*

**UNIVERSITY OF ILLINOIS PRESS**

*Urbana, Chicago, and Springfield*

Publication of this book is supported by grants from the University of Alabama's Office for Research and Economic Development, the University of Alabama's Collaborative Arts Research Initiative, the University of Alabama's College Academy of Research, Scholarship, and Creative Activity, and the General Fund of the American Musicological Society, supported in part by the National Endowment for the Humanities and the Andrew W. Mellon Foundation.

Library of Congress Cataloging-in-Publication Data
Names: Sargent, Joseph, 1970- author.
Title: Leo Sowerby / Joseph Sargent.
Description: Urbana : University of Illinois Press, 2024. |
    Series: American composers | Includes index.
Identifiers: LCCN 2023049018 (print) | LCCN
    2023049019 (ebook) | ISBN 9780252045936 (cloth) |
    ISBN 9780252056918 (ebook)
Subjects: LCSH: Sowerby, Leo, 1895–1968. | Composers—
    United States—Biography. | LCGFT: Biographies.
Classification: LCC ML410.S6882 S27 2024 (print) |
    LCC ML410.S6882 (ebook) | DDC 780.92 [B]—dc23/
    eng/20231018
LC record available at https://lccn.loc.gov/2023049018
LC ebook record available at https://lccn.loc.
    gov/2023049019

For my parents, Eugene and Patricia

# CONTENTS

# ACKNOWLEDGMENTS

THIS BOOK WOULD NOT HAVE BEEN possible without the support of many friends and colleagues. Among library and research staff members I am grateful to Nicole Westerdahl, Grace Wagner, Julia Chambers, Julia Dudley, and the staff of Syracuse University's Special Collections Research Center; Greg MacAyeal, Alan Akers, Dana Lamparello, and the staff of Northwestern University's Charles Deering McCormick Library and its Music Library; the staff of the Newberry Library; and Heather Gaunt, Ethel Villafranca, and Sarah Kirby at the Grainger Museum in Melbourne, Australia, for providing access to various primary source materials.

Francis Crociata, president of the Leo Sowerby Foundation, has been an invaluable resource for this project. From sharing various private scores, recordings, photographs, correspondence, and anecdotes to reading manuscript drafts and correcting several errors, he has gone above and beyond in supporting this biography. (Any remaining errors in the final version are of course my own.) Lorenz Maycher, the Leo Sowerby Foundation's vice president, was a gracious and generous host during my visit to the foundation offices in Kilgore, Texas, providing valuable access to archival materials, sharing a wealth of recordings and scores, and offering many stimulating Sowerby-related stories.

At the University of Alabama, generous financial support from the Office for Research and Economic Development, the Collaborative Arts Research Initiative, and the College Academy of Research, Scholarship, and Creative Activity has been crucial in supporting the research and publication process. Organist Faythe Freese and I co-taught a continuing education course on Sowerby through the Osher Lifelong Learning Institute, and I am thankful for the resources and anecdotes she shared about her Sowerby experiences. I am also indebted to Laurie Matheson at University of Illinois Press for her expert editorial guidance and to Gary Smith for his efficient organizational assistance.

*Acknowledgments*

I am especially grateful to the musicians and recording artists who agreed to be interviewed for this book. William "Pat" Partridge, Stephen Buzard, and Jim Ginsburg each offered fascinating perspectives on Sowerby's music, his personal character, and his continuing vitality in the twenty-first century. I have also benefited from conversations, advice, and support from various colleagues, students, and friends, including Bruce Ludwick, Frederick Teardo, Matthew Bogart, Christy Adams, Matthew Boyle, Don Fader, Gesa Kordes, Joanna Biermann, Linda Cummins, Jan Herlinger, Skip Snead, Sam Smith, and the anonymous readers engaged by University of Illinois Press.

I first encountered Leo Sowerby's music during my graduate student years, as a member of the Choir of Men and Boys at Grace Cathedral in San Francisco. I am deeply thankful to Ben Bachmann, Jeffrey Smith, Susan Hendrickson, Sue Crawford, and all my fellow choirmen and choristers from that period, for providing a wonderfully hospitable environment to absorb this repertory and for planting the initial seeds for this project.

# Introduction

## *Sowerby in American History*

**"IT IS NOT EASY AT THIS TIME WHEN MUSIC** is in so wildly kaleidoscopic a period of experimental change and innovation to try to assign a place in a historical sense to the music of Leo Sowerby."[1] This statement by Paul Hume, the longtime music editor of the *Washington Post*, appeared as part of a Sowerby tribute article in the October 1968 *Music: The A.G.O.-R.C.C.O. Magazine*, the composer having passed away the previous July at the age of seventy-three. Hume's tribute, one of ten included in the article, fell under the subhead "Organ and Choral Works"—the genres for which Sowerby remains far and away best known—yet it extends well beyond this framework, acknowledging both the rapid stylistic flux of contemporary American music writ large and the fading stars of former luminaries such as Sowerby, Walter Piston, Howard Hanson, and Roy Harris, whom Hume described as "products of an era that is now in partial eclipse."

But if Hume had a keen sense of America's shifting cultural tides, the prognostication at the end of his Sowerby tribute has proven somewhat less accurate: "I can see ahead only a steadily growing appreciation in widening circles of the best of Sowerby."[2] Among a select audience—most especially, organists and aficionados of music from the American Episcopal liturgical tradition—Sowerby's name continues to resonate, and a sense of "growing appreciation" might indeed be discerned for his organ and choral music, though acclaim for the composer is by no means universal. As for Sowerby's oeuvre outside the church, however, the circle has scarcely widened. For many twenty-first-century audiences, the partial eclipse of 1968 has become nearly total.

That such an eclipse shadows a composer who wrote more than 550 works across nearly all musical genres (notably excepting opera), and whose achievements include being the first American winner of the Rome Prize (in 1921) and garnering the 1946 Pulitzer Prize for music (for his cantata *The Canticle of the Sun*), is truly unfortunate. It often happens that a composer's legacy is ardently carried on by students and disciples of the immediately following generation, but struggles to extend beyond this point. In the case of Sowerby, advocates such as the organists Catharine Crozier, Ronald Stalford, and Robert Rayfield, pianist Gail Quillman, composer/conductor William Ferris, scholar/organist Ronald Huntington, Cedille Records president James Ginsburg, and especially members of the Leo Sowerby Foundation (Francis Crociata, Michael McCabe, Lorenz Maycher) have striven to maintain a level of visibility for the composer's music. But such efforts have faced challenges within an extraordinarily diverse modern musical landscape, and impressions of Sowerby now tend to coalesce into two different camps, depending on whether the context is sacred or secular in nature. In the church realm, Sowerby maintains a reputation as an "advanced" composer, writing complex organ and choral music that demands considerable skill and therefore discourages many performers. Stephen Buzard, music director at Chicago's Saint James Cathedral (where Sowerby himself worked for thirty-five years), related in 2017 an amusing anecdote in this respect. "As I tell colleagues of my plans to do a Sowerby recital tour and recording in 2018, their responses generally fall into one of two camps: 1. "I love Sowerby! He is the great American organ composer, etc." or 2. 'Why???'"[3]

As a secular figure, however, Sowerby presents more of a stereotypical "rise and fall" case, enjoying considerable renown in the pre–World War II era but later being perceived as outdated. Though sometimes labeled as dissonant and modernist in his own time, Sowerby remained committed to tonal procedures and techniques from earlier eras, even as experimentalist impulses increasingly captivated his peers. In discussions of the broader soundscape of early twentieth-century American composition, Sowerby is typically lumped into a grouping of "traditional" American composers alongside people like Hanson, Piston, John Alden Carpenter, and Randall Thompson, "who work along more or less conservative lines and make no attempt to write anything departing from general types of European music," as Henry Cowell put it as early as 1933.[4] Carol Oja has more recently aligned Sowerby with a group she has labeled the "forgotten vanguard"—composers who "envisioned an American modernist frontier but never fully crossed its borders."[5] "Conservative" and "neo-Romantic" are terms frequently applied to these figures, who maintained firm roots in tonality and embraced a range of older formal structures, which they often infused with distinctive "American" musical qualities, however that term might be defined.[6]

Sowerby's obscurity is all the more striking because, for long stretches of the earlier twentieth century, he was poised to take a leadership role in the American "vanguard." A precocious and largely self-taught composer, pianist, and organist, he came to public attention at age eighteen with a violin concerto that premiered with the Chicago Symphony Orchestra. From this point through the 1930s, his works featured regularly in the repertories of top American orchestras and chamber ensembles. The Chicago Symphony honored him with a highly unusual all-Sowerby concert in 1917, and he enjoyed a lengthy tenure as this symphony's resident composer. In 1921 he was named the first winner of the Rome Prize from the American Academy in Rome.[7] He went on to pursue a multifaceted career as a composer, keyboard soloist, teacher, and church musician, making outstanding contributions in each of these areas. His list of high-profile friends and associates was a long one: Frederick Stock, Serge Koussevitzky, Fritz Reiner, Eugene Ormandy, Pierre Monteux, Percy Grainger, Paul Whiteman, George Gershwin, Howard Hanson, William Walton, and E. Power Biggs, to name just a few. His sphere of influence encompassed many musicians who would later achieve renown—Ned Rorem (1976 Pulitzer Prize winner), Gail Kubik (1952 Pulitzer Prize winner), Florence Price (first African American woman to be recognized as a symphonic composer), and William Ferris (first American composer to teach at the Vatican, among other achievements) all count among his former students.

Certainly the most distinctive aspect of Sowerby's career was his devotion to the church, an area in which he stands head and shoulders above his peers. He had been an organist at various churches since his youth, and at age twenty-four he garnered a professional position as associate organist at Fourth Presbyterian Church of Chicago. Later he moved to Saint James Episcopal Church (now Cathedral) in Chicago, becoming music director in 1927, while simultaneously teaching at the American Conservatory of Music. Becoming confirmed as an Episcopalian the following year, he remained at Saint James until 1962, when he became the founding director of the College of Church Musicians at Washington National Cathedral. Sowerby's choral and organ music earned for him considerable success, leading to his being deemed "the dean of American church musicians" by his contemporaries even as his concert works gradually lost the popularity they had once enjoyed.

Today, Sowerby's music remains something of a niche enterprise. Scholarly analysis of the repertory is largely confined to master's theses and doctoral dissertations, many of which are by now several decades old, though select pieces like the orchestral tone poem *Prairie* (1929) and the cantata *The Canticle of the Sun* (1945) have received notable recent attention.[8] Program notes from recordings often represent the most substantial written commentary on a given piece, particularly for instrumental works in the concert realm.[9] In view of Sowerby's lengthy career across a wide panorama of sacred and secular musical life, a more extended study of his music and his place in American cultural history seems long overdue. Such are the twin tasks of this book, the first published biography of Sowerby. It endeavors to bring disparate audiences together in considering Sowerby as a "complete" composer—not simply a sacred specialist, or a rise-and-fall concert figure—and removing some of the obscurity that has surrounded his achievements.

This process, however, leads to the inevitable realization that Sowerby can be difficult to pin down. Although certain portions of his career emphasized sacred or secular works to various degrees, it would be improper to label Sowerby as either a strictly sacred or a strictly secular composer. Indeed, conventional labels of any sort tend to be problematic; during his own lifetime Sowerby was variously called a liberal, a conservative, an anarchist, a traditionalist, a mystic, and a nationalist.[10] Sowerby himself acknowledged these contradictory reactions, having once remarked, "I have been accused by right-wingers of being too dissonant and cacophonous, and by the leftists of being old-fashioned and derivative."[11] He went so far as to call himself "a musical Dr. Jekyll and Mr. Hyde," symptomatic of his interest in various genres and styles across both sacred and secular realms.[12]

Such diverse judgments are in part a result of Sowerby's patent refusal to align himself with a particular school of compositional thought. On numerous occasions, he made clear his aversion to labeling himself stylistically. In commentary published in John Tasker Howard's 1941 volume *Our Contemporary Composers: American Music in the Twentieth Century*, he claimed to have a penchant for "not thinking about my style, or idiom, trying constantly to improve my techni[que], so that when I shall have something to say, I shall be able to say it clearly and directly, and—God willing—simply."[13] An even more direct expression of these sentiments came shortly before his death in 1968, when he stated, "I would be completely stumped if I had to write a piece in the style of Sowerby . . . for I don't know, and don't exactly want to inquire too carefully, as to what that style is."[14] According to Robert Rayfield, a Sowerby student and longtime organ professor at Indiana University, Sowerby's compositional practice was simply to "set down what he felt and heard."[15]

Sowerby's refusal to define himself by a particular label or brand likely made him complicit in his own later reception difficulties. Sowerby was never much interested in promoting his own music; his introverted nature and quiet demeanor were incompatible with the aggressive pursuit of performance, publishing, and recording opportunities. As the organist E. Power Biggs remarked shortly after Sowerby's death, "Meeting L[eo] S[owerby], you would not suspect him to be the highly imaginative and original genius that he was."[16] This reticence may have also contributed to the fact that several of Sowerby's scores are now lost, making promotion an even more challenging task.

Burnet C. Tuthill, a fellow composer, conductor, and writer on music (as well as the son of William Burnet Tuthill, the architect of New York's Carnegie Hall), offered the following portrait in 1938 as part of a lengthy assessment of Sowerby's life and music.

> Sowerby is red headed and spunky, but not in an aggressive way. On the contrary he is soft spoken and shy to avoid large gatherings even where the meeting of many persons similarly interested in music would promote a greater interest in his works. If a musical convention is to meet in his home city of Chicago, he will most likely take a train in the opposite direction and visit with his close friends. To these he is intimate and cordial; but even with them he is most reticent in displaying his latest creation or some work which has lain on his shelf for many years awaiting a performance. His shyness in this respect has contributed to the delay in the general acceptance of his compositions. His work as a choirmaster, organist, and teacher occupies the greatest portion of his time.[17]

In developing a portrait of Sowerby, this book draws upon primary source materials from various collections, including especially Syracuse University, Northwestern University, the Newberry Library in Chicago, Washington National Cathedral, and the Leo Sowerby Foundation in Kilgore, Texas. Together these collections offer an exhaustive range of correspondence, photographs, memorabilia, news clippings, published scores, unpublished manuscripts, and private recordings, further exploration of which could someday yield an even more richly detailed study. I also consulted several academic theses and other writings containing firsthand recollections from Sowerby himself or from those close to him, though some of the primary source documentation itself no longer survives.[18] These latter volumes present substantial outlines of the major people, places, and events of Sowerby's career, along with a profusion of anecdotes, interviews, and other narratives.

Fundamental to the present portrait are questions of musical style, and each chapter spotlights a select group of pieces that exemplify various aspects of Sowerby's compositional thinking. Several discrete stylistic phenomena can be associated with Sowerby's music: a pervasive emphasis on complex chromatic harmonies within a tonal framework; an abiding interest in orchestration and tone color; vigorous engagement with jazz and folk materials; an aversion to the atonal and avant-garde impulses of certain of his peers; and particularly in his sacred music, the adaptation of English models to an American context. Special attention will be given to Sowerby's organ music, a vast repertory in which the composer pushed the boundaries of performance technique in a manner that belies quite pointedly the "conservative" label often attached to him. (Indeed, one might reasonably question whether those who dismiss Sowerby as old-fashioned have any familiarity at all with his organ pieces.) Although Sowerby enjoyed a lengthy publishing relationship with H. W. Gray Company, and more recently the Leo Sowerby Foundation has printed a number of works from his concert repertory, many of his works remain unpublished and unrecorded, necessitating hands-on engagement with original manuscripts.

Another through-line involves Sowerby's engagement with issues of "American" character. Amid the divergent perspectives shaping early twentieth-century debates on the proper direction of American music, Sowerby regularly engaged with this issue in his own music. Many of his compositions reference American life overtly, whether in drawing on specific folk tunes for melodic inspiration or in developing programmatic portraits of American life. Such "place pieces," as Denise Von Glahn has emphasized, convey crucial information about America's evolving cultural identity as well as composers' own sense of self-identity, in ever-changing manifestations across an enormous landscape.[19] Other composers and critics, meanwhile, identified various qualities in Sowerby that purportedly bespoke of his "American" nature, thoughts that were further developed (by Sowerby himself as well as these observers) in newspaper articles, journals, concert reviews, and other publications. An American consciousness even extended into his church music, where his achievements were viewed as pioneering in terms of developing a distinctively native sacred style (most notably in their references to jazz/blues sonorities and modal/chromatic harmonies) and advocating for higher quality music within American liturgies.[20] Collectively, these materials present a valuable opportunity to consider Sowerby's self-identification as an American composer, as well as to reengage with broader ideas on twentieth-century American musical consciousness. A truly comprehensive treatment of this subject would involve navigating a diffuse theoretical landscape on nationalism that extends beyond the scope of this volume; the approach taken here is to collect a range of commentary from Sowerby, his audiences, his critics, and others in his circle, and then to extrapolate from this evidence an understanding of how American qualities were perceived within this circle, the nature of these qualities, and the ends for which the qualities were cultivated.

Through all this activity, understanding Sowerby's place in musical history becomes a complicated endeavor. To appreciate his impact on American music necessitates considering both secular and sacred perspectives, which might have substantially divergent aesthetic priorities; what might be considered conservative to a secular audience could be quite radical in a liturgical context. This perspective also stands in contrast to much Sowerby research to date, which tends to address him as *either* a church music composer *or* a concert composer. A more integrated approach to the composer may not fully resolve the contradictory labels that have been attached to his name, but hopefully it will move us forward in terms of gaining an appreciation for this multifaceted and multitasking figure.

Chapter 1 focuses on Sowerby's early life (1895–1918), emphasizing his prodigious early development, formative experiences as pianist, composer, and organist, and burgeoning interest in carving out a position for himself on the American musical scene. It explores Sowerby's early interest in folk music both American and otherwise, from "The Irish Washerwoman" to his early orchestral piece *Three British Folk-Tune Settings*. Stylistic analyses of early works showcase a range of qualities: the youthful, sometimes brash ambition of his Violin Concerto; the folksy charm of "The Irish Washerwoman"; the evocative tone painting in his organ repertory (*Comes Autumn Time*); a willingness to be provocative in terms of harmonic language (*A Set of Four: Ironics for Orchestra*).

Chapter 2 considers Sowerby's young adulthood (1919–27), highlighting his early symphonic successes in Chicago and beyond as well as his budding relationships with important artistic figures and patrons, most notably Frederick Stock and the Chicago Symphony Orchestra. It traces the features of Sowerby's modernist musical language through a selection of exemplary pieces (the Violin Sonata No. 2 in B-flat, the symphonic poem *From the Northland*, the gargantuan *Psalm Symphony*) and explores his increasing distaste for certain currents of international avant-garde modernism, exposure to which came especially during his three years in Rome as the inaugural winner of the Rome Prize. Sowerby's organ music, which the composer himself categorized into three periods (though these strict demarcation lines should be taken with a grain of salt), is addressed with a consideration of the first "orchestral period" (exemplified by *Carillon*), which, in employing registrations that emphasize the organ's ability to produce various orchestral colors, presents distinct parallels with Sowerby's symphonic engagement.

This chapter also develops several core ideas on American music as understood within Sowerby's particular circle, among contemporaries who were not part of his circle, and by modern scholars of American music.[21] Early in his career, Sowerby composed many works whose musical substance bears obvious associations with American culture, through devices such as folk melodies and jazz harmonies/rhythms as well as explicit extramusical imagery that connects the music with the American physical and cultural landscape. Sowerby's writings on this subject further emphasize an early belief that native melodies were essential for any composer's formation of individual identity.

Chapters 3 and 4 consider Sowerby's lengthy career in Chicago (1927–40 and 1940–62, respectively) and his continuing relationships with patrons, students, and peers. These chapters trace the shifting nature of his engagements with both concert music and church music, through documentary evidence of Sowerby's dual careers as music director of Saint James Church Cathedral and as a professor of harmony and composition at the American Conservatory of Music. The perspectives of chapter 3 are rooted in the idea of a gradual focus shift, in which Sowerby now balances sacred and secular musical activities more equally by relinquishing his activities as a concert pianist and composing more liturgical music for organ and/or chorus. In terms of organ music, the chapter charts what are commonly identified as Sowerby's second and third stages of development. The second stage is a "pure organ period" (1931–38), in which concert works display less concern with orchestral color.[22] A focus on two of Sowerby's most popular organ pieces, the Symphony in G Major (often considered his *magnum opus*) and *Pageant*, illustrates this more "pure" focus. What has sometimes been called a third stage, though which may be simply a subset of the pure organ period, has been labeled a "Baroque response" (1939–68), reflecting parallels with the neo-Baroque *Orgelbewegung* period of stripped-down registrations and lower wind pressures, as well as Sowerby's own heightened interest in Baroque compositional techniques (as exemplified in his *Toccata*). Sowerby's body of services and canticles, through which he sought to supply sufficient music to cover the entire church year, shows how he adapted features of English sacred style in an effort to formulate an original American idiom, as exemplified by the Magnificat in D Major. This chapter also considers Sowerby's growing identification with the city of Chicago, and how his status as a midwestern composer played into negative prejudices of the New York/Boston crowd, as evidenced by stark differences in his reception by composers, critics, and audiences from these areas.

As Sowerby's standing grew in Anglican and other sacred milieus, chapter 4 takes up the idea of balance turning into imbalance, with sacred music increasingly dominating his activities. Musical analysis of works for the concert hall (Symphony No. 3, *The Canticle of the Sun*) focuses on Sowerby's continued exploration of core elements that were long characteristic of his style—an emphasis that says much about his own musical integrity, but one that also became increasingly problematic in terms of maintaining critical interest amid rapidly changing fashions. This chapter explores the reasons behind Sowerby's steady disappearance from concert hall stages, from Sowerby's own attitudes to the various and often starkly contrasting perceptions of peers and critics. Sacred musicians, meanwhile, increasingly acknowledged Sowerby as the foremost figure in American church music, and analysis of representative organ and choral works (*Arioso*, Psalm 122 "I Was Glad When They Said unto Me") shows how Sowerby consolidated his position as a premier composer of complex, evocative religious works. This chapter also explores more fully Sowerby's role as a musical statesman, assessing his philosophies on church music and his perceptions of modernism as they apply to both sacred and secular repertories.

Sowerby's efforts to preserve a legacy of American sacred music, as evidenced by his late compositions, his final years in Washington, DC, and his involvement as director and composition teacher for the newly established College of Church Musicians (CCM), form the centerpiece of chapter 5. This chapter, covering the last years of Sowerby's life (1962–68), explores his attachment to Washington as well as the history and development of the CCM. It scrutinizes his late writings on church music and particularly on the education of church musicians, a recurring refrain in his public commentary, and discusses how these attitudes were translated into the CCM curriculum. It also considers the implications of the CCM project, which, though lasting only seven years, produced a number of high-caliber church musicians. Examples of his late music (the cantata *La Corona*, the anthem "Thy Word Is a Lantern unto My Feet") show a still-vibrant compositional impulse as well as a determination to solidify his legacy as a composer of note.

A brief epilogue considers Sowerby's reception history in America and addresses several recent efforts to revive Sowerby as a public concert figure, incorporating firsthand commentary from leading figures in these initiatives. As referenced at the beginning of this introduction, Sowerby has endured a somewhat mixed reception in the decades following his death. His devotion to manifold older techniques in concert music contributed to a conservative reputation that boded ill for his later reception, yet among church musicians he is often viewed as an advanced, complex composer, whose popularity is limited not by a sense of being old-fashioned but by being too challenging for mainstream institutions. These contrary impulses give rise to questions of whether Sowerby's artistic status has been unjustly denigrated based on his deep association with church music, and whether scholars have unfairly dismissed Sowerby for not being sufficiently "art"-focused in his outlook. And indeed, this dichotomy between forgetting and remembering may have additional implications beyond the case of Sowerby, speaking to broader presumptions about what a twentieth-century American composer ought to have composed to be deemed worthy of remembrance.

# The Emerging Americanist (1895–1918)

I



SOWERBY HAS OFTEN BEEN DEFINED NOT SIMPLY as an American composer, but as a midwestern one. There are several good reasons for this. Two of his most acclaimed concert works (*From the Northland: Impressions of Lake Superior Country* and *Prairie*) take direct inspiration from this region's landscapes. Most of his own career was spent in Chicago, and throughout his life his strongest supporters tended to come from this city as well. Sowerby himself repeatedly referenced his midwestern roots in printed commentary, and critics from both the Midwest and beyond latched onto this geographic identity when assessing his music.

Many aspects of Sowerby's "midwestern-ness," including his own consciousness of this as part of his compositional identity, emerge from his earliest years. His childhood was spent in Michigan, while his advanced schooling occurred in Chicago. Several of the most influential early figures in his life, from conductor Glenn Dillard Gunn to composer Percy Grainger, espoused nationalist musical ideals, which Sowerby adapted to his own framework. Though he certainly drew plenty of inspiration from beyond the Midwest as well (and indeed beyond America), the first inklings of his interest in American and other folk idioms—ideals that are fundamental to his compositional thinking—stem from these formative years.

Sowerby's early development might further be considered from the perspective of being a child prodigy. Though Sowerby lacked certain qualities of classical music's most famous prodigies (the international travels of Mozart, the economic and intellectual advantages of Mendelssohn), notions of prodigy do arise in terms of his early manifestations of deep talent, youthful concert successes, and insatiable hunger for musical growth. If he did not ultimately develop a status akin to Mozart or Mendelssohn, documentary and anecdotal evidence points to him being an unusually focused child, quickly absorbing whatever resources were at hand and eagerly pursuing his ambitions.

## Early Life and Family

Leo Salkeld Sowerby was born May 1, 1895, in Grand Rapids, Michigan. His father, John, was a postal worker, foreman of the mailing division at the United States Post Office.[1] His mother, Gertrude, died when Sowerby was four years old while giving birth to a second child, who also died. Both sides of Sowerby's family had roots in England, his father having emigrated from Cumberland (now part of Cumbria) at age three and his mother's family also having a Cumberland lineage by way of Ontario, Canada. After Gertrude's death, John married Mary Wiersma, a widow whom he had hired to be a housekeeper, on October 15, 1901. Mary had at the time a fourteen-year-old daughter, Bertha Wiersma Nolton, who thus became Leo's half-sister.

In interviews from the early 1970s, both Bertha Nolton and Leo's cousin Lillian Sowerby offered various insights into Leo's early life and upbringing. Bertha remarked that the Sowerbys' home life was satisfying throughout Leo's childhood and that John and Mary enjoyed a happy marriage; in her words, "I don't think two people ever married that were happier together than [Leo's] father and my mother."[2] Leo's father, John, according to Bertha, was "the most gentle, most wonderful man. You couldn't ask for anything better"—a sentiment confirmed by Lillian, who stated, "[Leo's] father was what you would call gentle by nature, rather quiet, as I think Leo was." Mary, meanwhile, "did everything and anything that Leo wanted" according to Bertha, though Lillian also observed that she could be strict with him.[3]

As for Leo himself, Bertha stated: "He wasn't healthy when I first met him. My mother saw to it he got outdoors, had a sled, and became a normal boy. Leo was not particularly arresting as a small child, but he did become better looking as he grew older. Of course, as he developed, that intelligence just shone out of his face. Freckled face, red hair and it just stuck up straight—my mother used to put coconut cream on it to hold it down."[4]

Leo took up the piano at age seven, at the encouragement of his stepmother Mary and despite concerns from his father that he was too frail to play the instrument.[5] Both his mother Gertrude and his stepsister Bertha had also played piano, and Mary in particular encouraged Leo's early musical interests and ensured a regular practice routine.[6] He studied with Ida Bundy for about three years and then, starting at age ten, with Mrs. Frederick A. Burton, through whose direction he began to gather attention in local public performances. One such performance occurred with the Grand Rapids Furniture City Band on March 18, 1906, at which Sowerby played Gottschalk's *Last Hope* and Beethoven's Sonata No. 6, Op. 10, No. 2. His "debut" as an organist, meanwhile, occurred at his graduation from grammar school, at which he played "America" on the pedals.[7]

According to Lillian, Leo was an eager music student who regularly performed for relatives and neighbors. "He was quite gracious in playing for members of the family. . . . When he visited us, we had an organ and not a piano, but he was very willing to play for some of our friends. Since we had told them that he was a musical prodigy, almost, they wanted him to come into their homes and play. He did it very willingly."[8] His early piano studies included popular as well as classical music, and Sowerby recalled playing one song, Neil Monet's "Hiawatha, a Summer Idyll," so often that it instilled in him a permanent aversion to popular music—a precursor to the elevated artistic ideals he would maintain so vigilantly in his later life.[9]

Sowerby's compositional inclinations emerged in tandem with his piano study. Sowerby "was studious and industrious right from the beginning," according to Francis Crociata, and he knew by age eight that he wanted to become a composer.[10] Bertha recalled that Sowerby "would write on the floor in front of the fireplace, then jump up and go try it out on the piano and would come back. Or he had a small table that he would draw up to the piano stool and turn from one to the other."[11] The earliest known Sowerby composition, composed around age eight, was, according to Bertha, "a little waltz that Leo wrote while lying on the floor in the living room in front of the fireplace" and dedicated to Bertha herself.[12] Sowerby had little formal training during these years and was essentially self-taught as a composer, learning in part from a harmony textbook that he borrowed from the library in Grand Rapids.[13]

By 1909, however, it was clear Sowerby needed more advanced study than what could be had in Michigan. With the encouragement of his teacher Mrs. Burton, the now fourteen-year-old Sowerby moved to Chicago—the city that would become the focal point of his life—for further study in piano, harmony, and composition. Originally selected for a scholarship at the Chicago College of

Leo Sowerby as a boy (Courtesy of the Special Collections Research Center, Syracuse University Libraries).

Music, but dismayed at the thought of having a female teacher, Sowerby instead attended Englewood High School and studied piano and harmony with Calvin Lampert, the organist at Chicago's Westside Christian Science Church. During these years Sowerby lived with a widow named Jessie Louise Nolton (who was Bertha Nolton's mother-in-law) and her son William.[14]

By his own admission Sowerby was something of a loner, rarely socializing with either his Englewood classmates or with Lampert's other students.[15] Instead he spent his time in the Nolton home, with regular visits from his stepmother and occasional trips to visit family members such as his stepaunt, who lived across town and at whose house he would sometimes "dress up and give acts of Shakespeare."[16] His father also sent him regular packages from Michigan, and he returned home for summer vacation during his early Chicago years. Sowerby was otherwise preoccupied with his musical studies, which included conducting practice in the bedroom of the Noltons' maid—the only available room with a mirror—though ironically he took no actual music courses at Englewood.[17] In this light it is unsurprising that he quit high school after the eleventh grade, despite being a good student academically (though this fact did not prevent him from later being awarded a master of music degree from the American Conservatory of Music, in June 1918).

Sowerby's teenage years in Chicago were marked by prodigious development as a pianist, organist, and composer. His harmony and composition studies with Lampert lasted only four months, as Lampert quickly realized that Sowerby's talents demanded more than he could offer. While continuing to teach Sowerby piano, he passed along compositional instruction duties to Arthur Olaf Andersen, a faculty member at the American Conservatory who had studied with Vincent d'Indy and who would become one of Sowerby's most ardent supporters. As a piano student, meanwhile, Sowerby proved so talented that Lampert stopped accepting payments after the first year, stating that the honor of teaching Sowerby was payment enough.[18]

Sowerby quickly gained renown for his pianism, at the American Conservatory and across Chicago. Under Andersen's guidance, and thanks to his own highly developed technique, he found himself in increasing demand for performances in various solo and chamber recitals during 1911 and 1912.[19] In 1913 he added to this experience a pair of recitals back in Grand Rapids, on January 12 with the Furniture City Band and an April 8 recital at Saint Cecelia Auditorium, where he played two of his own songs ("With Strawberries" and "The Full Sea Rolls and Thunders"), along with a piece by Andersen.[20]

Alongside his piano activities, Sowerby turned his attention to the organ. Inspired by an experience in 1910 turning pages for pianist/composer Clarence Loomis, who had played a César Franck organ piece during an American Conservatory ensemble class, Sowerby purchased the sheet music for Franck's Choral 3 in A Minor and set his mind toward learning the piece.[21] Although Lampert gave him six lessons on the instrument, Sowerby's organ study was essentially self-directed, and one of the most commonly shared Sowerby anecdotes relates to this self-training. Having first struggled to secure practice time at Chicago's Old South Congregational Church, due to a recalcitrant sexton who refused to believe someone as young as Sowerby could be serious about the organ, Sowerby soon faced the additional obstacle of not being able to afford the church's twenty-five-cent practice fee. In response, he developed a novel solution: obtaining a large sheet of brown wrapping paper from a butcher shop, he sketched out the organ's pedal board upon it and placed it on the floor beneath his piano, affording him a makeshift device on which to develop his foot technique.[22]

Sowerby secured his first professional organ job in 1913, as a substitute organist at Grace Episcopal Church in Oak Park during the summer and, later in the year, for three months as organist for Bethany Union Church. He also continued to absorb repertory, developing a special fondness for the music of Max Reger. One subject that failed to capture Sowerby's interest, however, was organ construction and design. As late as 1953 he remarked that he had "no interest in mechanical aspects of the instrument and has never drawn up an organ specification"—a remarkable admission from someone who would ultimately achieve such prominence for his organ repertory.[23]

Among the fruits of Sowerby's compositional labors during the early 1910s was a Trio in the Form of a Sonatine in A Major for piano and two violins, presented at a program with other Andersen students in a March 11, 1911, recital. A review by C.E.W. in *Music News* heralded Sowerby as something of a prodigy: "Leo S. Sowerby was the best pianist on the program and . . . his compositions excelled all others in the instrumental line. One could quarrel a little with the over-brilliance of the piano scoring of his 'sonatina,' but his slow movement was so very greatly better than the others, and the general form so much more compact and adhesive, that the question of excellence settles itself, and in performance he was splendid."[24] This was followed by a December 16, 1911, performance of American Conservatory students featuring Sowerby's Trio in D Major, the only student work on the program.

## First Major Exposure

Sowerby scored his first major public appearance as a composer in 1913. Glenn Dillard Gunn, a conductor and music critic for the *Chicago Tribune*, hired the Chicago Symphony Orchestra (CSO) for two performances of new American works and invited the eighteen-year-old Sowerby to contribute a violin concerto. Sowerby wrote the Concerto for Violin in G Minor in sixty-three days, and the first performance occurred on November 18, 1913, with Herman Felber (Sowerby's friend and the orchestra's youngest member at the time) as soloist. The audience response was enthusiastic, and while critics gave the concerto mixed reviews, they were encouraging about Sowerby's potential. Maurice Rosenfeld of the *Chicago Examiner* noted that Sowerby had "decided creative talent," while faulting the concerto for excessive length and noting its stylistic resemblance to Claude Debussy.[25] Adolf Brune of the *Chicago Inter Ocean* echoed these critiques, but nonetheless declared the concerto a "pronounced success" and called Sowerby "greatly endowed by nature."[26] Most effusive of all was the *Chicago Tribune*, which called Sowerby "the surprise of the evening" and praised the concerto as "wonderfully brilliant in its passages, broad in its treatment, ever original—a veritable musical prophecy."[27]

The Debussy connection is intriguing in view of the fact that Sowerby's teacher Andersen was a disciple of d'Indy, who (contrary to popular opinion) admired Debussy's impressionist music.[28] Like many figures of his generation, Sowerby was drawn toward French composers including Franck and Debussy, with a special reverence for d'Indy. In a January 1915 letter to the *Chicago Music News*, written in response to a review of *Eight Little Pieces* for cello and piano that criticized him for being a "futurist" in the manner of Arnold Schoenberg or Anton Webern, Sowerby claims that "of course, I have studied carefully the Schoenberg scores . . . but so have I studied those of d'Indy, Reger and others, and surely, if I felt it compatible with artistic standards to 'imitate,' there would be none better to copy than d'Indy, assuredly the greatest living composer."[29]

"Debussyian" qualities can be read into several features of the violin concerto. The slow introduction features languid opening melodic fragments atop slow, sustained pedal chords, establishing what critics likely construed as the work's impressionist nature. Abundant chromatic harmonies and recurring thematic patterns also seem to recall Debussy's nonfunctional harmonic vocabulary and motivic manipulations, even as Sowerby's tonal centers appear with greater regularity. The concerto is further framed as a single, continuous movement with wide-ranging moods, a contrast to the genre's traditional multimovement structural plan.

Gunn had hired the CSO out of a belief that American orchestras were not often enough performing the works of native composers—an issue keenly highlighted by an incident during one rehearsal in which he spoke about the necessity of performing music by Americans, but the German musicians couldn't understand him because they were accustomed to rehearsals in the German language.[30] He went so far as to establish his own American Symphony Orchestra in 1915, populated entirely by American musicians and playing only American repertory, though the project was abandoned in 1917 when nearly half of its musicians were drafted into the army for World War I. Sowerby's concerto was not particularly patriotic in content, but his association with this event and his status as an up-and-coming composer thrust him into the conversation about American music—a subject he would address more directly in both music and words across the next decade.

Following the CSO premiere, Sowerby resumed a vigorous schedule of performance and compositional activities. In 1914 he inquired about taking organ lessons with Eric DeLamarter, an organist and composer who had recently accepted a position at Chicago's Fourth Presbyterian Church. Sowerby knew DeLamarter through connections with the CSO and Jessie Nolton, and DeLamarter (who like

Sowerby's composition teacher Andersen had trained in Paris) would become one of his closest friends and mentors.[31] He auditioned for DeLamarter with Bach's "Cathedral" Prelude and Fugue in E Minor, and DeLamarter responded with an invitation for Sowerby to perform several recitals on Fourth Presbyterian's Ernest M. Skinner organ, telling him, "you don't need lessons, you just need a chance to play and be heard."[32] The first of these recitals, on August 26, 1915, illustrates Sowerby's striking ambition in terms of tackling imposing repertory by Bach, Camille Saint-Saens, d'Indy and others, including his own *Madrigal* as well as a piece by DeLamarter, *Intermezzo*. Earlier that spring, Sowerby had also secured a regular organist position at Old South Congregational Church—the same church where he had once struggled to schedule practice time.

During these years Sowerby also made several appearances in Chicago and Grand Rapids, as both pianist and composer. Among the more notable engagements was an April 7, 1914, recital with Felber, sponsored by Gunn, featuring a piece by DeLamarter—a triumvirate of important Sowerby relationships during this time. Just twelve days later, Gunn presented another recital in which two other performers debuted Sowerby's Sonata for Violin and Piano in E Minor, which the *Chicago Daily Journal* termed "fully as interesting as his violin concerto . . . less sketchy and more sustained."[33] Other Sowerby works performed in recital include his first organ work (the chorale-prelude *Rejoice, Ye Pure in Heart*), several solo songs, a Magnificat, and *Eight Little Pieces* for cello and piano. Sowerby also began speak publicly on musical matters, with four lecture-recitals at the Grand Rapids Ladies Literary Club in October-December 1914, and four additional lectures at the Grand Rapids home of Mrs. William S. Rowe during February-April 1915.

Gunn's CSO concerts from the 1913–14 season had been successful enough that two additional performances (entitled "American Music with Americans") were programmed for 1914–15. At the second of these, on March 11, 1915, Gunn and the CSO premiered Sowerby's tone poem *Symphonic Sketch: Sorrow of Mydath*, on a text by English poet John Masefield. Sowerby had completed the piano sketch on January 9 of that year, with the orchestration finished just five days later on January 14.[34] As with his earlier violin concerto, reviews tended to praise Sowerby's novelty while faulting his abundance of content. Rosenfeld called the piece "originality run riot" and stated there were "many good spots in the work, but it needs critical surveillance, and a blue pencil."[35] Another critic took this opportunity to offer an aggressive salvo in the battle to define American music, stating that such music "cannot find any vital inspiration in Negro, folk or Indian melodies or in so-called rag-time rhythms" but is rather found in someone like

Sowerby, "the great hope for the young American composer" in terms of blending existing European models into an original American amalgam.[36]

As it happened, this particular critic's vision of Sowerby's future would not be entirely fulfilled. Though Sowerby certainly drew heartily on European influences, folk and jazz elements would also soon find a prominent place in his music. On March 10, 1916, Percy Grainger—a composer well known for his devotion to folk music—made his debut with the Chicago Symphony Orchestra, as piano soloist for Edvard Grieg's Piano Concerto and the world premiere of John Alden Carpenter's Concertino for Piano and Orchestra. News of this visit attracted the attention of Sowerby, who in a letter dated February 28, 1916, introduced himself to Grainger with a mix of humility, flattery, and self-deprecating humor.

> My dear Mr. Grainger,
>
> There is no justification for the liberty I am taking in writing to you beyond the fact that I should like to presume to show you a group of settings of three Somerset folk tunes I have made for piano, when you come to Chicago, if you are not to be completely occupied with other and more important things. The tunes I have used, and also the tunes I have taken for an orchestral Rhapsody, which is to be played here this week are some which I jotted down at recitals given by the Sisters Fuller. Perhaps because of the fact that these healthy straightforward tunes find in me an ardent devotee, I am an enthusiast on the score of Mr. Percy Grainger's compositions and piano playing, too. At any rate, I should be pleased if you might let me know if you will have any time to see me and to poke fun at my pieces.
>
> Sincerely,
> Leo Sowerby.[37]

The "Sisters Fuller" refers to a touring English trio who performed and collected folk songs. Sowerby had attended multiple performances of theirs in early 1915 at the Chicago Little Theatre and, entranced by what he heard, proceeded to write both his orchestral *Rhapsody on British Folk Tunes* (1915; the premiere Sowerby mentions in his letter was with Gunn's American Symphony Orchestra on March 2, 1916) and *Three Folk-Tunes from Somerset* (1916) for piano.

Subsequent to this letter, Sowerby traveled to New York in summer 1916 for a brief period of piano lessons with Grainger, which in reality were more like bull sessions where the two composers played and discussed their favorite music. From these sessions Sowerby obtained among other things an appreciation for the music of Grainger's friend Frederick Delius, whose well-known orchestral *Florida Suite* would find an analogue many years later in Sowerby's *Florida Suite* for piano. (In later years, Sowerby claimed that Delius was the composer whose style he felt closest to himself, and that the proper way to perform Sowerby's own music is similar to how the conductor Thomas Beecham approached Delius—not choosing an overly fast tempo, and giving the pieces time to unfold.)[38] Grainger and Sowerby remained friendly over the succeeding decades, frequently exchanging letters in which they discussed wide-ranging professional and personal matters, from rehearsals and performances to social visits.

In view of Grainger's well-known racist leanings, it is natural to ponder whether Sowerby shared any of these unfortunate perspectives. From a documentary standpoint, there are no direct indications that Sowerby espoused discriminatory racial practices. He certainly never expressed anything as patently offensive as John Powell's program notes on *Rhapsodie Nègre* (1918),[39] and despite his friendship with Grainger there is no overt evidence that Sowerby supported his "blue-eyed English" mentality.

One letter from Sowerby to Grainger deserves examination in light of a 1920s campaign by Grainger to promote specifically Anglo-Saxon music. In this letter, dated March 16, 1924, Sowerby writes, "You do not need to be assured of the sympathy I feel for the idea of giving concerts of Anglo-Saxon music, and I am most grateful to you for asking me for some of my works for the program."[40] Does this remark imply support for Grainger's own prejudices, or does it reflect more simply an interest in promoting his own music and that of other American composers? Grainger's campaign was a distinctly personal mission (Sarah Kirby has recently argued it "can be seen as rather self-serving, in that Grainger was using the music of his friends not for their own individual artistic merits, but to present an aesthetic element to his own, quite idiosyncratic political and ideological viewpoint"), and there is no direct evidence that Sowerby was aware of its political or racist undertones.[41]

Another consideration is that Grainger's biases were directed most strongly against central and southern Europeans, especially Italians and Austrians, whereas Sowerby—who at the time of the abovementioned letter was nearing the end of a three-year residency in Rome—took pains to learn the Italian language and to develop friendships with Italian performers and composers (some of whom he wrote about in correspondence with his friend Lorry Northrup).

A further counterweight is Sowerby's regular support of figures from underrepresented demographics, whether they were women and/or African American. His early connections with female musicians included violinist Amy Neill and pianist Winifred Christie; later in life, one of the major exponents of his organ music was the leading American organist Catharine Crozier. The composer Florence Price was one of Sowerby's notable students at the American Conservatory, and the limited documentary evidence of their relationship suggests a supportive

Sowerby with Winifred
Christie playing a
Bechstein-Moor piano
(Courtesy of the Leo
Sowerby Foundation).

attitude overall. A single surviving letter from Sowerby to Price, responding to her request for information about the National Association for American Composers and Conductors, indicates at least some measure of support for Price's ambitions.[42] His choir at Saint James Cathedral included an African American singer named Jess Brodnax, who was reportedly very fond of Sowerby, and one of the finest organists to study at the College of Church Musicians was another African American, Garnell Copeland. Sowerby's racial attitudes may have been more or less typical for his time—perhaps not especially enlightened from a twenty-first-century standpoint, but lacking any undue sense of prejudice or hatred.

Musically, Grainger's influence can be seen in Sowerby's piano setting of the country dance tune "The Irish Washerwoman." Composed in 1916 and issued as his first published composition, this piece highlights Sowerby's burgeoning interests in colorful sonorities, textural variety, and harmonic complexity. The inspiration for this piece came from an unlikely source: an Irish maid named Fannie Regan, who worked for Jessie Nolton in Chicago. Exasperated by Sowerby's continual practicing of works by classical masters, she reportedly exclaimed one day, "Why don't you play something decent?" When Sowerby asked what kind of music she meant, the response was, "Faith, and a good tune is the Irish Washerwoman. Ye'd do some good playin' the likes o' that."[43]

In an extended letter to his former composition teacher and mentor Karl Klimsch, written (but never actually sent) between 1902 and 1904, Grainger outlined several aspects of his personal musical outlook, including a predilection for texture, emotional impact, and purity of style over such features as form, instrumentation, and technique.[44] Other ideals commonly associated with Grainger's aesthetic include the idea of "sameness" when setting folk tunes and eschewing common ideals of development and structure. In a 1916 essay about musical progress entitled "The World Music of To-morrow," Grainger addresses modern composers' attraction to folk music, stating that when he and others set folk tunes, "I am convinced we do so, not so much because of our close affinity with primitive music, but, on the contrary, because we relish enormously the dramatic clash of the archaic non-harmonic folk tune with our own overflowing harmonic exuberance."[45]

Sowerby's approach to "The Irish Washerwoman" falls in line with many of these ideals. Though presenting the folk tune in myriad configurations and with various ornamental details, the melody itself is never fundamentally altered. The piece also resists precise formal definition or thematic development; it is not a theme and variations, nor does it employ other common variation techniques such as chaconne, passacaglia, or ground bass. Sowerby's chief priority seems to be heightened emotional impact, achieved via diversity of harmony, tempo, texture, and overall mood. This is discerned most keenly in the evocative expressive markings used to mark various statements of the melody ("with spunk and very lively," "sneakingly," "clanging," "with broader sweep," "clingingly," "quietly and flowingly," "jerkily," "very crisply," "energetically," "swinging along in big style," "faster, with ginger"). Grainger, for his part, knew this setting well enough to include it among a list of superior recent American repertory compiled in 1919—pieces in select genres (piano solo, piano and voice, choral music) "that have stirred and thrilled me the most deeply within the past year or so—in the hopes that these gems of native creativity will bring to some of my fellow musicians (who are not yet familiar with them) the same delight and inspiration that they have brought to me."[46]

## Further Study, Composing and Concertizing

Throughout 1915 and 1916 Sowerby continued to concertize with abandon, while maintaining his composition study under the tutelage of Andersen and beginning to attract notice from figures outside his immediate circle. Chamber performances as a pianist in Chicago and Grand Rapids continued apace, as did his organ recitals at Fourth Presbyterian. He further produced a variety of chamber works (a suite for violin and piano, a serenade for string quartet, a woodwind quintet), solo songs, organ chorale preludes, a set of *Portrait Sketches for Piano*, a two-piano adaptation of *Sorrow of Mydath*, and *Homage to England's Country Folk* (a reorchestration of *Rhapsody on British Folk Tunes*). Also dating from 1916 is his first choral work, "The Lord Bless Thee," a short responsory for soprano soloist and choir. This year also marks the moment when Sowerby began smoking cigarettes, a habit that would notably impact his health in later years.

Another piece from this period emerged from rather unusual circumstances. DeLamarter had planned to include a new Sowerby piece for his Fourth Presbyterian organ recital on Thursday, October 26, 1916, but evidently failed to mention this fact to Sowerby himself, who only discovered DeLamarter's plans upon reading a recital notice in the previous Sunday's *Chicago Tribune*. Thus placed dramatically under the gun, Sowerby crafted *Comes Autumn Time* in a single afternoon on Tuesday, October 24, basing the piece on a poem by Bliss Carman, "Autumn," which he had seen in the newspaper. DeLamarter premiered the yet-untitled piece (appearing in the program as "From the Southland," a dummy title DeLamarter himself devised) with barely any rehearsal time.

Nature features prominently throughout Carman's poetry, and "Autumn" is teeming with vibrant images of natural phenomena, fused with exotic references and carried by a lyrical flow.

> Now when the time of fruit and grain is come
> When apples hang above the orchard wall,
> And from the tangle by the roadside stream
> A scent of wild grapes fills the racy air,
> Comes Autumn with her sunburnt caravan,
> Like a long gypsy train with trappings gay
> And tattered colors of the Orient,
> Moving slow-footed through the dreamy hills.
> The woods of Wilton at her coming wear
> Tints of Bokhara and of Samarcand;
> The maples glow with their Pompeian red,
> The hickories with burnt Etruscan gold;
> And while the crickets fife along her march,
> Behind her banners burns the crimson sun.

Sowerby responds to this poem with his own colorful depictions, cast within sonata form. The very first gesture is a burst of fireworks, a triumphant A-major main theme in the pedal set against rapid-fire arpeggios in the manual that are gradually infused with chromatic harmonies. The excitement of this opening section vividly evokes the flowering harvests associated with Autumn's "sunburnt caravan." Yet before long Sowerby's theme becomes fragmented and the energy subsides, yielding to slower rhythms and more unstable harmonies. A languid second theme emerges in the dominant E major against a relaxed ostinato accompaniment, portraying the slow-moving gypsy train. Quick-shifting registrations in this section provide an aural analogue to the train's various exotic Oriental colors. Both themes are then developed with harmonic complications; fragments of the first melody are presented in minor, inversion, and transposition, while the second also appears in various transpositions and is at one point directly intermingled with the first theme. A recapitulation of the first theme brings back the fireworks, leading to a presentation of two statements of the second theme's opening strain. Motives from the first theme then reappear as part of a brief but triumphant closing stretch.

Besides showcasing Sowerby's ability to blend programmatic references with traditional formal structures, *Comes Autumn Time* exemplifies what is known as the "orchestral period" of Sowerby's organ compositions, the first of three stages as defined by Sowerby himself.[47] Repertory from this orchestral period emphasizes tonal color and quick registration changes, emulating the sonic variety of the symphony orchestra—"not the orchestra of the Viennese Classics, but that of the French Impressionists," according to Sowerby's student Robert Rayfield.[48] And indeed, Sowerby extended this approach literally by crafting his own orchestrated version of *Comes Autumn Time*—a task he completed on December 16, 1916, for a special all-Sowerby orchestral performance on January 18, 1917, by sixty members of the Chicago Symphony. Organized by DeLamarter and sponsored by Sowerby's friend and patron Walter Douglas Main, a munitions manufacturer to whom he had dedicated "The Irish Washerwoman," the concert also included an orchestrated version of "The Irish Washerwoman" (completed just days earlier on January 6) along with *The Sorrow of Mydath*, concertos for both piano (with soprano soloist) and violoncello, *Three Somerset Tunes*, and a *Ballade on Song Themes*, an arrangement by DeLamarter of Sowerby tunes.

This concert was a high-water mark in terms of Sowerby's visibility, though perhaps inevitably for a twenty-one-year-old, critical reaction to the music was decidedly mixed. Multiple reviewers faulted Sowerby for a lack of coherence and direction, though others praised his handling of folk themes and orchestral color, and Rosenfeld in particular predicted that Sowerby, "properly developed, should become one of America's foremost composers."[49] The performance was also semi-

Program for all-Sowerby concert with the Chicago Symphony Orchestra, 1917 (Courtesy of the Special Collections Research Center, Syracuse University Libraries).

nal in terms of consolidating Sowerby's relationship with the CSO and particularly its music director, Frederick Stock, who attended the concert and thereafter became an ardent Sowerby supporter. Stock invited Sowerby to compose a piece for the CSO's next season (to which he responded with *A Set of Four*, more on which below), and other Sowerby supporters began speaking more openly about the composer's prowess, as indicated for instance by DeLamarter's comments in *Musical America*: "Judgments on young composers are apt to be deceptive. I might name some who would not live up to their present promise. But I think I may safely name Leo Sowerby . . . as a composer of tremendous promise. He has a wealth of fantasy and a facile technique to express it."[50]

Around this time, Sowerby decided to have a summer cottage built in Palisades Park, Michigan, midway between Chicago and Grand Rapids. Andersen had provided him with the plot of land, and the cottage was finished in August 1917.

For decades afterward, this getaway would serve as a favored locale for intensive composition activity. In the meantime, he produced his first cantata, *A Liturgy of Hope*, for soprano soloist, choir, and organ (using Psalm texts on themes of conflict and hopefulness, resonating with the strife associated with World War I), though it was not premiered until March 15, 1928.

Sowerby's performance career, meanwhile, continued to blossom. In a February 14, 1917, concert with four CSO string players (billed as the Chicago Piano Quintet) he premiered his *Tramping Tune*, which he described as "a description of political rally time, off-key bands, street corner haranguers, a stirring come-along spirit"—an augury of both the United States' imminent entry into World War I and Sowerby's personal patriotism. The quintet gave a repeat performance on February 25 as part of what would be the American Symphony Orchestra's final concert, and Sowerby also appeared in this performance as soloist for his piano piece *Prelude and Toccata by Purcell*. In June he traveled to Connecticut to perform at a festival sponsored by the Litchfield County Choral Union, at which he reunited with Grainger, and later that month gave another organ recital at Fourth Presbyterian. It was also at this time that Sowerby first became associated with the American Conservatory as a piano teacher, while continuing to study composition with Andersen.

Sowerby joined the US Army on December 8, 1917, having previously been rejected on account of poor eyesight (exotropia), and was stationed at Camp Grant in Rockford, Illinois. His final compositional endeavor before enlisting was to arrange *Tramping Tune* for band, a deliberate effort to obtain a musical military assignment—specifically with the 321st Machine Gun Battalion, where the band-master was a friend of his. The ploy worked, in part. After a stint in basic training that included coal shoveling, potato peeling, and horse grooming, Sowerby was indeed assigned to a band, but a lower-quality one: the 332nd Field Artillery, for which he was handed a clarinet—an instrument he didn't actually play.

Surviving correspondence with Percy Grainger and with Lorry Northrup, a lawyer and close personal friend, offer intriguing firsthand details of his army experience. Sowerby tells Grainger about his initial disappointment at not being assigned to the 321st battalion, but later speaks well of his work with the 332nd ("the band work continues to be very interesting; we are now getting down to some real work, and I fancy the band sounds better than it really is").[51] In another letter he references the 332nd band performing Grainger's "Irish Tune" and "Shepherd's Hey" ("I like the arrangements *ever so much*") and talks shop about band arrangements, praising both Grainger himself and the French style ("they write for band as one would for an orchestra").[52] He even wrote a song for the battalion, *Three-*

Title page for score of *332, F.A.*, 1919 (Music Library, Northwestern University, Evanston, IL).

*Three-Two, F.A.*, with words by Capt. Louis E. Legner, which was published in both piano and band arrangements.

Not long after enlisting, Sowerby obtained leave to attend the CSO's February 15–16, 1918, premiere of his *A Set of Four: Suite of Ironics*. This was an orchestrated version of five piano-cello duets, dedicated to DeLamarter (for whom the duets were originally written) and crafted in response to Stock's earlier invitation. Sowerby had originally hoped to write a larger-scale original piece for Stock, but time was not on his side; as revealed in a letter to the composer Daniel Gregory Mason, "this wasn't at all the thing I wanted to do for Mr. Stock . . . however, time was getting short, and I saw the army business looming up ahead, so I dropped the idea of this bigger thing."[53]

Crociata has observed that this piece embodies a kind of teleological stylistic narrative, moving from high Romanticism to a modernist vein.[54] It thus proves a useful vehicle for considering how Sowerby, as a composer still in his early twenties, perceived the progression of his own modernist language. The slow first movement, wistful and subdued, maintains a firm sense of expressive tonality. Repetitive, lyrical melodies and enriched harmonies (with a particular fondness for consecutive half-step motion) permeate the overall fabric. This leads to a brisk second movement that borrows from the Grainger playbook: a lively folklike theme, introduced first in solo piccolo and then a solo violin, permeates the movement and is frequently reworked through fragmentation and transposition. Rapid shifts among instrumental groupings, quick repetitive gestures, and regular alternation between duple and triple meter supply the movement's kinetic energy. Rhythmic complication also permeates the serene third movement, in ternary form. In the A section, a languid solo viola melody lies beneath two different ostinato patterns, one duple and one triple, while the pastoral B section is set in 5/8 meter. The vigorous final movement revisits the folk idiom, as Sowerby infuses his lively melodies with chromatic twists, abundant reiterative gestures, and quick motivic changes.

As a snapshot of Sowerby's developing modernist sensibilities, *A Set of Four* reveals several priorities. Folklike melodic content is now extended into an abstract realm, beyond the more literal earlier setting of "The Irish Washerwoman." Sowerby's melodies may lack precise national or cultural identifiers, yet their liveliness, brevity, and frequent repetition nevertheless convey a sense of regional character. To these melodies Sowerby adds a range of devices including rhythmic vigor, systematic motivic repetition, and chromatic/dissonant harmonic interest, complicating their presentation though never abandoning their tonal frameworks.

Chicago critics responded more positively to this piece than they had to the earlier violin concerto. The *Chicago Examiner* hailed the "young soldier composer who brought a novel thrill" to the concert, while the *Chicago Journal* praised Sowerby's new brevity and his ability to control the "unexpected quirks and tricksy turns" in his music.[55] Two separate reviews specifically identified a connection to Grainger, the *Chicago Daily Tribune* calling Sowerby the "most gifted of the Grainger adulents" and the *Chicago Herald* stating, "In his 'Set of Four' he paid a call at the villa belonging to Mr. Grainger, one of those latter-day originals whose art possesses the exuberance and the vivaciousness which well might be expected to fascinate a composer whose years are comparatively few."[56]

When the piece was later performed in San Francisco, however, its playful elements aroused some controversy, as reported by *Musical America*.

> Three contending parties developed: The cognoscenti, who recognized the fine technical equipment of the composer and the deftness with which he had turned modern tendencies as well as the staid rules of composition to the end of humor; the tyros, who insisted

Sowerby in uniform at Bordeaux, France, 1918 (Courtesy of the Grainger Museum collection, University of Melbourne).



stoutly and verbosely that the work transmitted all the aural irritation of a battle in a barn-yard; and the public, who, feeling their heels titillated by Mr. Sowerby's presentation of jazz in the process of reduction ad absurdum, enjoyed it—and said so.[57]

The weekend CSO performances happened to coincide with Sowerby's being promoted to the rank of third-class musician, though the events were not directly related. (An amusing anecdote relates to this coincidence, with Sowerby's commanding officer startled to read a newspaper review of his CSO success just one day after he granted Sowerby the promotion.) Further promotions quickly followed, to sergeant (April 1), bandmaster of the 322nd (April 21), and then second lieutenant (August 21). The last promotion coincided with Sowerby's unit sailing to France, thanks to a new policy that American bandmasters serving abroad were automatically granted equivalent ranks to other allied nations. Sowerby was stationed at Camp de Courneau (near Bordeaux) for six months, a period that included a three-week sojourn to England. He had hoped to visit Delius during this trip, though ultimately he did not do so until the summer of 1927. His journeys included a visit to Winchester Cathedral, perhaps a foreshadowing of his later deep interest in the English cathedral music tradition.

Sowerby was honorably discharged from the army on February 28, 1919, and thereafter he regarded his time in the military with great reverence. In a letter to Grainger and his mother, written in Newport News, Virginia, immediately upon his arrival from France, he proclaimed, "the experience I've had in the army will always be worth much. And it has been enjoyable in a musical way as well as others."[58] Later in life, when reflecting on this period, Sowerby claimed his military experience was vital in terms of learning how to live with others and that its resonances remained influential.[59] And as a specifically musical memento of his experience, in 1920 he composed the organ piece *Requiescat in Pace*, inscribing on the manuscript "In Memory of Our Dead—1918."

Understanding Sowerby as an American composer entails more than just perusing scores and identifying folk melodies, because his notion of America was not simply musical. Sowerby was a patriot in many ways, and the formative experiences of his youth and early adulthood were essential to his burgeoning notion of being both an American artist and citizen. This identity would be further consolidated in the coming years, with international travels, heightened exposure to global trends, and the emergence of jazz all helping to shape his perspectives.

# Home and Away

## *European Travels, American Concert Success (1919–27)*

**THE POSITION OF AMERICAN CLASSICAL MUSIC** in the post–World War I era has been the subject of wide-ranging and sometimes divisive discussion. On one hand, composers of this period often enjoyed heightened institutional support of their music. They were buoyed by a sense of patriotism fueled by the United States' involvement in war, along with a concomitant disdain for all things German. The *New York Times* recognized this fact even in the midst of wartime, observing in October 1917 that "American composers have their innings this year and for this the war is directly responsible."[1] An ensemble like the Chicago Symphony, which only recently had been so infused with German personnel that it conducted rehearsals in that language, now faced a gap in terms of seeking out non-Germanic repertory—a gap that Sowerby and other American composers endeavored to fill with alacrity. On the other hand, some observers have viewed this period in more problematic terms. Joseph Horowitz has provocatively termed the postwar era "the great schism," a time in which a culture of performance, dominated by superstar performers/conductors and the institutions that supported them, enshrined canonic works while sublimating artistic creativity, leaving many composers on the sidelines.[2]

Across these divergent interpretations, one unassailable fact is that composers of the period pursued extremely varied stylistic paths. Carol Oja has described the immediate postwar era as a time of great flux for American composition, "with no way of knowing which composers and aesthetic visions would get left in the historiographical dust."³ Some figures chose to extend traditional formal models and aesthetic values, building on the approaches of Second New England School composers. Others emphatically rejected these traditions in favor of different ideals: "newness, experimentation, even audacity," in Oja's words.

Sowerby is sometimes aligned with the former group, as someone whose music is overshadowed by the modernist experimentalists. But if he never pursued the more radical impulses of figures like Henry Cowell or Edgard Varèse, he was nevertheless far from a mere derivative. Indeed, throughout this decade Sowerby developed a distinctive style that caused many observers to view him as something of a provocateur. He also developed contacts with high-profile patrons and began to appear more frequently on national stages, while further bolstering his place among Chicago-area institutions as both composer and pianist. His music during this period continued to explore folk and jazz idioms, in certain cases taking these to greater extremes, while developing an advanced harmonic vocabulary within the framework of tonality.

Another important aspect of Sowerby from this period is his emerging status as a commentator and musical authority, expressing in print his thoughts about modernism and the question of "American" musical style. In contrast to some other composers, for whom nationalism can be associated with discrete historical, political, commemorative, or other qualities of the homeland, Sowerby's sense of America was rooted in personal experiences of the nation during his current times. It was also shaped by deliberate comparisons (both positive and negative) with other national traditions: an urge to move beyond traditional German models in concerted music, as well as an impulse to draw on Anglican sacred music for inspiring parallel movements in America. A more local American context additionally emerges in Sowerby's strong identification with the city of Chicago, as opposed to the traditional American cultural hubs of New York and Boston, invoking notions of center and periphery in terms of understanding what particular "American" qualities were desirable in music.

## Return to Chicago

Upon concluding his army service in 1919, Sowerby returned to Chicago and immediately resumed a full battery of creative activity. He took up residence with his former composition teacher Andersen, with whom he had continued to study intermittently before the war. He quickly found gainful employment with two churches, becoming organist-director at Wellington Avenue Congregational Church as well as DeLamarter's associate organist-director at Fourth Presbyterian. Wellington Avenue boasted a brand-new organ, dedicated in December 1917, upon which occasion Sowerby had earlier composed his *Introit for Advent*.[4] In his new position he now continued to compose and give organ recitals, including a recital on November 11, 1920, that featured his own *Comes Autumn Time* and *Requiescat in Pace*.[5]

At Fourth Presbyterian, meanwhile, Sowerby quickly made several contributions. His first composition upon returning to the States was an ambitious anthem, "The Risen Lord," on texts from the Lutheran hymn "Christus ist erstanden" and Charles Wesley's "Hymn to the Trinity." Set for antiphonal choir and solo SATB quartet, it was dedicated to the Fourth Presbyterian choir and performed by them on Easter Day (April 20, 1919). Two other anthems written this same year and published in 1920 were "The Lord Reigneth" and "I Will Lift Up Mine Eyes," the latter of which—a lyrical setting for alto soloist, choir, and organ featuring lush, chromatic harmonies—remains one of Sowerby's most popular works. Sowerby also gave four consecutive weekly recitals on the church's E. M. Skinner organ in June and July 1919, featuring several newly composed works (*Madrigal*, *A Joyous March*, *Carillon*) as well as music of both Andersen and DeLamarter.

*Carillon* demonstrates Sowerby's continued preoccupation with orchestral color, which was doubtless abetted by the particular specifications of Fourth Presbyterian's organ. (Skinner was known for building symphonic-style instruments with several new stops.)[6] It also displays such telltale stylistic features as harmonic complication, repetitive gestures, formal integrity, and learned devices. Cast in a kind of modified sonata form, without development but with coda, the piece opens with a languid, descending melody and an accompaniment permeated by chromatic half-step motion. The second theme, in the subdominant, presents the work's first "carillon" effect: a series of short repetitive gestures, registered for celesta (or flutes as a substitute), atop continued chromatic accompaniment (see example 1). A reprise of the first theme follows, and then the carillon theme recurs in the home key but with two new configurations: canon in the manuals and augmentation in the pedal, the latter of which is registered for chimes (a regular feature of Skinner organs). Although Sowerby distanced himself from *Carillon* later in life as not being representative of his mature style, the piece has endured as a wistful, picturesque evocation of sonic color.

Having quickly reestablished contact with his closest mentors after the war, Sowerby also began to extend his professional network outwardly. This was not necessarily a comfortable maneuver, as Sowerby's modest nature militated against such promotional activities, yet his concert profile rose precipitously in these years.

Example 1. *Carillon*, H.134, mm. 30–41

From April 29 to May 2, 1919, he conducted the Minneapolis Symphony Orchestra in his *Three British Folk-Tune Settings*, as part of an Illinois Music Teachers' Association program. Two weeks later, the Chicago-based Shostac String Quartet performed his *Songs for Contralto with String Quartet*.

Later in 1919 he received a chamber music commission from Elizabeth Sprague Coolidge, a pianist and arts patron who had recently established the Berkshire Festival of Chamber Music in Pittsfield, Massachusetts, and whom he had previously met two years earlier (dedicating to her his *Serenade in G Major* for string quartet [1917]).[7] His lively Trio for Flute, Viola, and Piano premiered there on September 26, 1919, to a favorable review from the *Berkshire Evening Eagle*, which quotes one observer who called the piece "the happiest music he had heard in a long time."[8] Another American composer on the program, Daniel Gregory Mason, bore witness to Sowerby's status as an emerging provocateur:

Mason and Sowerby had engaged in regular correspondence throughout 1917–18, with Sowerby sending Mason various scores and Mason working to promote Sowerby's music, while also expressing frank criticism at times (which Sowerby accepted humbly).[10] Mason was a staunch adherent of German Romanticism, trained by members of the Second New England School, and he had little patience for French impressionism or other modernist trends despite having recently studied in Paris with d'Indy. If one might therefore take his distinctively form-forward emphasis with a grain of salt, his remarks are nevertheless important in illuminating Sowerby's increasing centrality to discussions of emerging American composers.

From May 30 to June 6, 1919, Sowerby dramatically shortened and revised the piano concerto that had originally premiered at the January 1917 all-Sowerby CSO concert (and which originally had a wordless soprano line, inspired by a Ferruccio Busoni piano concerto where a male chorus appears in the fifth movement), in preparation for a new performance with Stock and the CSO. He worked on scoring at various points in July, September, and October 1919, finishing the piece on October 8. Now dedicated to Coolidge, the concerto premiered on March 5–6, 1920, to favorable reviews that cemented Sowerby's status as a major American talent. W. L. Hubbard penned an article in the *Chicago Daily Tribune* whose title made the case clear: "America Will Lose Its Greatest Composer If Sowerby Goes Abroad." Responding to rumors that patrons were advocating for Sowerby to study abroad in Paris—the undisputed fashionable mecca for young American artists—Hubbard proclaimed, "Music lovers of America should petition the government to deny to Leo Sowerby any passport that permits him to leave the confines of this country during the next ten years. . . . Here is the biggest and most remarkable creative musical talent we have yet had."[11]

Sowerby with Percy Grainger (*left*) and others, Pittsfield, Massachusetts, 1919 (Courtesy of the Leo Sowerby Foundation).

In program notes to a later performance from December 29, 1925, at New York's Aeolian Hall, Grainger offered a snapshot of the piano concerto's musical substance, calling it "full of its writer's always very genuine musicality, with an engaging and typically American flavor of vitality in its gay sections, of sensitiveness in the slow movement. On the technical side it evinces a delightful characteristic that we have learned to expect from Sowerby works for whatever combinations; an almost Berlioz-like exceptional facility for extracting from each instrument, or group of instruments, those sounds most truly native to it." Many of the livelier sections indeed evince a certain folklike character, permeated with sprightly melodies, snappy rhythmic bursts, and pianistic effects; the affinities to Grainger's own folk-inspired works of this period (*Molly on the Shore, Shepherd's Hey, Handel on the Strand*) are unmistakable. Yet the concerto also bears more individual Sowerby hallmarks: chromatic complication, abundant repetitive gestures, and a multimovement form that embraces a continuous succession of material rather than the typical fast-slow-fast scheme.

Sowerby was markedly conscious of his rising status in the national art music scene, perceiving his concerto as both forward-thinking and unmistakably American. In a letter to Coolidge shortly after the premiere he proclaimed, "A bomb was most certainly fired into the ranks of the 'old guard.' . . . It pleased me to learn that so many musicians who heard the Concerto regarded it as a really American expression, for that is what I most wished to convey in it."[12] The piece also became one of his most important calling cards over the next several years. Grainger conducted the work later that year in Aeolian Hall, and Sowerby himself performed it with the Minneapolis Symphony, Tri-City Symphony, St. Louis Symphony, and Berlin Philharmonic, as well as a repeat performance with Stock and the CSO on December 27, 1924.

March 1920 brought a second important boost to Sowerby's reputation when Boston Music Company published the orchestral version of *Comes Autumn Time*. This piece quickly thrust Sowerby onto the national scene, being taken up by the orchestras of Philadelphia, Chicago, Minneapolis, Los Angeles, Detroit, and Baltimore in 1920 alone. *Musical America*, in lauding Boston Music Company for publishing a large-scale American orchestral work like this, termed Sowerby one of the country's "most forceful creative personalities."[13]

Throughout 1920 and 1921 Sowerby continued to raise his profile, appearing in chamber and orchestral performances in Chicago and beyond as both pianist and organist. He appeared in promotional advertisements for the Mason and Hamlin piano company and for the singer Ora Lightner Frost, through whom he solicited bookings for an upcoming tour (which however never took place). He was a co-winner of the Society for the Publication of American Music's 1921 composition contest with the *Serenade* he had dedicated to Coolidge. In July–August he participated with nine other American composers in a large-scale 300th-anniversary celebration of the Pilgrims' landing at Plymouth, Massachusetts, composing for the occasion the choral "Recitative and Pilgrim's Chorus" (also arranged for concert band, though the score and parts are now lost). As a sign of his increased presence in society circles, he was inducted on May 1, 1921, into the Cliff Dwellers, a Chicago men's club for professional artists and connoisseurs with which he would enjoy a four-decade-long association.

Another oft-repeated anecdote attesting to Sowerby's reputation emerged around this time. At the end of September Sowerby attended the fourth Berkshire Festival in Massachusetts, at which both his woodwind quintet and his Suite for Violin and Piano were performed, the latter by Sowerby himself along with violinist Léon Samatini. Sowerby was one of only three composers, along with Bach and Beethoven, to have two works on the program. This fact, along with Sowerby's increasing reputation for pungent chromatic color, prompted either the flutist

Georges Barrere or the librarian/musicologist Oscar Sonneck (depending on the source) to supply a new answer to the age-old question of which composers are regarded as the "three Bs" of classical music: "Bach, Beethoven, and Sower-B!"[14]

In tandem with this growing artistic visibility, Sowerby began to speak more openly about his perspectives on American music and on current modernist trends. Infused with the anti-Germanic sentiments of his age, Sowerby strongly rejected Teutonic models in favor of new nationalist paths, even as he acknowledged the difficulty of identifying a true "American" music. A revealing profile published in the February 12, 1921, edition of *Musical America* outlines several of his priorities, bearing a title ("Apathy Drawing Us Back under Foreign Domination, Says Sowerby") that speaks to a growing sense of urgency on the subject. "The danger menacing American musicians is foreign domination," Sowerby asserts in this article. "We must be free to develop American music as an expression of American ideals, and not be continually expected to pour our ideas into ready-made molds of old-world manufacture."[15] Sowerby assails foreign and especially German "propaganda" as hindering the development of national idioms. He also casts some blame on the American public, for both their apathy and their determination to measure American composers against foreign standards.

Such remarks, taken at face value, might paint Sowerby as some kind of radical firebrand. Looking more critically at his music, however, it is evident there were limits to how far he sought to depart from older forms. Indeed, one striking aspect of Sowerby's modernist perspective is his marked hostility toward the avant-garde, and the strength of his conviction that tradition was a necessary foundation for any composer's development. In categorizing his fellow modern composers, for instance, he describes first "the group of utter radicals, of sensationalists, whose little vogue is rapidly passing. They have added nothing that the world needs, for they have no sound foundation for their work." A second group, "governed by general historic traditions of music," encompasses Sowerby's favored figures: the modern French school, Grainger, Cyril Scott (a composer Grainger himself supported ardently), and "most of the sincere American composers. . . . Their work is not different basically from that of the old school. If it were, I wouldn't think it had the right to exist."

Given the myriad challenges facing American classical music, what materials should be used to craft a national identity? The issue is especially problematic for Sowerby because America lacks the unified folk song tradition of many other countries. "Neither Indian nor Negro themes can be the basis of the best music" in his view, as the former in particular suffers when melodies are outfitted with classical harmonies. What Sowerby identifies instead are certain ineffable qualities that increasingly coalesce around America: "a spirit of hopefulness, cheerfulness, and good-will, which is often boisterous and rather uncouth." And there also exists a truly American music in the form of jazz, an idiom Sowerby likes personally but believes needs refining before being deemed suitable for art music. "I like it, if it is clever. In the really joyous freedom of jazz music lies its lesson for composers. But it needs very thorough pruning and refining, and needs the hand of an artist to shape it into a real expression."

## The Rome Prize

Sowerby having now attracted notice on the national stage, it was perhaps inevitable that an international residency would soon follow. As early as 1918 Sowerby had inquired to d'Indy about studying with him in Paris; d'Indy's response, dated January 11, 1919, indicates a willingness to arrange lessons should he ever make his way across the ocean.[16] But as it turned out, the focal point of Sowerby's international experience would be Rome instead of Paris. In 1921 the American Academy in Rome (AAR) added a musical composition department to its curriculum and launched an annual competition for a three-year Prix de Rome fellowship.[17] The first competition attracted fourteen applicants, but the six-member committee (including John Alden Carpenter and Walter Damrosch as judges) was not satisfied with any of them. Felix Lamond, an organist and enthusiastic AAR advocate who became the first professor of music in Rome, then personally bestowed the award upon Sowerby despite his not having been an applicant. (Howard Hanson, one of the original fourteen candidates, was soon afterward granted his own fellowship when Lamond insisted the committee reconsider the applicant pool.) Also helping Sowerby's case were Elizabeth Sprague Coolidge and other Chicago patrons, many of whom had connections with AAR supporters and who had already been nurturing his career in various ways.[18]

Sowerby departed for Rome on November 3, 1921, accompanied by Lamond and his wife. Originally slated for a two-year residency, Sowerby exercised an option to extend his tenure by a year, remaining in Europe through October 1924. The Rome Prize came with many benefits: sumptuous work accommodations in the beautiful Villa Aurelia (and later in the even more expansive Villa Chiaraviglio) atop one of Rome's highest hills, the Janiculum; opportunities for fellows' music to be performed by both Rome's orchestra and a resident quartet; a concert series featuring both traditional and new music; and other perks such as monthly musical receptions, personal and travel stipends, and music copying/publication subventions. In letters to Coolidge, Sowerby wrote appraisingly of the many opportunities to connect with other types of artists, to travel throughout Europe (which he was permitted to do for up to six months every year), and to absorb the latest stylistic trends.[19]

Sowerby took full advantage of his surroundings. His compositional output from this period includes more than a dozen works for sundry orchestral, chamber, solo, and choral forces, which were performed at more than twenty concerts, in Rome and across Europe.[20] He established lasting friendships with a range of performers (Mario Corti, Amy Neill, Lynnwood Farnam, Carlo Zecchi), composers (William Walton, Herbert Howells, Ottorino Respighi, Mario Castelnuovo-Tedesco, Enrico Bossi), and conductors (Antonio Pedrotti). Hanson, who joined Sowerby in February 1922, became a close friend and remained one of his important advocates in the succeeding decades. Sowerby's international travels during this period included visits to London, Belfast, Paris, Berlin, Vienna, Salzburg, Trento, Torino, and many other locales. In England he attended the Three Choirs Festival three years in a row (in Gloucester, Worcester, and Hereford respectively), as well as the Leeds Music Festival in 1922. Sowerby also enjoyed absorbing Italian culture and learning the language, getting by with his command of French until he could speak Italian with some fluency.

All this exposure afforded close contact with modernist developments across Europe and helped sharpen Sowerby's own aesthetic perspectives, which were

Pencil sketch of Sowerby from the American Academy in Rome (Courtesy of the Special Collections Research Center, Syracuse University Libraries).

often quite different from the music he was hearing. He certainly appreciated the necessity of composing with an up-to-date sensibility, as evidenced for instance by the aforementioned 1921 *Musical America* commentary. When it came to the more radical European practices, however, he was markedly less sanguine. A flash point in this respect was the Internationale Kammermusikaufführungen in Salzburg, August 7–10, 1922, a major undertaking that led to the founding of the International Society for Contemporary Music, an organization still active and prominent to this day. Sowerby and violinist Corti premiered his Violin Sonata No. 2 in B-flat at the festival, dedicating the work to Lamond. Afterward, he expressed his strong antipathy toward the program's more avant-garde repertoire.

> The German, Austrian and Hungarian music at this international music festival was simply unbelievably awful, the most ugly, brutal, rackety and disgusting stuff I ever heard; there is no question that they have absolutely finished musically—but they don't know it. We had a tremendous dose of it too. There was twice as much middle European music as there was of all the other music put together. They are all trying to go Schoenberg one or two better, and the results are, to say the least, appalling. Songs by [Ildebrando] Pizzetti, [Mario] Castelnuovo and [Gian Francesco] Malipiero were, I am glad to say, some of the best successes of the programs, while a work by Arthur Bliss, a young Englishman, pleased me greatly.[21]

A comparison of excerpts from two works on the program vividly illustrates these differences in approach. The first movement of Sowerby's violin sonata traverses myriad moods, from a lovely, songlike opening to moments of liveliness and "blue notes" reminiscent of jazz. Example 2a, taken from early in the movement, illustrates Sowerby's continued interest in cultivating folk characteristics. Though not specifically labeled as American or folk, the sprightly melodies, lively rhythms, gentle syncopations, and occasional flat-seventh sonorities could fit comfortably within an American folk song. Edwin Evans, in reviewing the Salzburg festival for the *Musical Times*, deemed the sonata "the only hundred percent American work," though his actual opinion of the piece was mixed.[22]

Compare this with an excerpt from the first theme of the first movement of Béla Bartók's Sonata No. 1 for violin and piano (example 2b), also performed at the festival after premiering earlier that year in London. Though also rooted in a folk idiom (David Cooper views this opening violin melody as a stylized version of a Hungarian dance called the *verbunkos*) and ostensibly bearing a tonal orientation of C-sharp minor, Bartók's brash dissonance, intervallic leaps, and bold transformations of the folk material may well have embodied the "ugly, brutal" qualities Sowerby described.[23]

Sowerby was not the only American to criticize the festival repertory. Upon returning to Salzburg the next year for the first "official" festival of the newly

Example 2a. Sowerby, Violin Sonata in B-flat, H.165, mvmt. 1, mm. 38–46

Example 2b. Bartók, Violin Sonata No. 1, Sz75, mvmt. 1, mm. 1–7 (*continues*)

Example 2b. *Continued*

established International Society for Contemporary Music, he was now joined by Hanson, Lamond, and Randall Thompson, the 1923 Rome Prize winner. Lamond, responding to what was billed as a "path-breaking" program of works by Alban Berg, Schoenberg, Bartók, Igor Stravinsky, and others, summed up the Americans' reactions by decrying this music as "heart-breaking" and lacking in beauty.[24]

Given all this rhetoric, there is something of an irony to the fact that Sowerby's music back home continued to spark accusations of radical tendencies. After the Chicago Symphony premiered his Symphony No. 1 on April 7–8, 1922, a savage anonymous review in the *Musical Herald* took the composer to task for his "jumble of sounds," which were further labeled as "bizarre." The reviewer describes Sowerby as "a good bit of a genius, but who, if permitted to go his own way without curb, might prove dangerous to himself and his young colleagues. According to older and wiser people, Mr. Sowerby is a musical radical veering toward unmusical socialist. . . . The composer is young, and unless he rid himself of his anachronisms he had better hie himself to France, where the unruly, unconventional 'Six' are holding high jinx [*sic*] with their polyphonic free love."[25] A more thoughtful review, by composer Felix Borowski in the *Boston Evening Herald*, adeptly pointed out Sowerby's debts to Grainger and proclaimed the composer to be "clear[ly] on the side of modernity," describing his music as having a "devilish cleverness" and that "often it has shocked or irritated the average listener"—although ultimately his personal opinion of the symphony was decidedly mixed.[26]

Besides granting exposure to wide swaths of current European repertory, Sowerby's Rome years served to reaffirm his own identity as an American composer. In a letter to Coolidge written shortly after departing from America, he made clear his intent to maintain a national sensibility while in Rome, even as he understood the necessity of absorbing European styles. "I am going to work hard to keep my head right where it belongs on my shoulders, and to remain a good and real American, in spirit, as in fact. But I know I shall get in Europe from its wealth of tradition, the very thing I could never get here."[27] He also took the even bolder step of aligning himself specifically with Chicago, a city that to his mind most completely embodied the nation's values and culture. In comments from early 1923 to Edgar Ansel Mowrer, a Rome-based correspondent for the *Chicago Daily News* who later won the Pulitzer Prize for his reporting on Adolf Hitler's rise in Germany, he proclaimed that "I consider Chicago my home. . . . It is our largest and most interesting, thoroughly American city." To these remarks Mowrer himself added that, though Sowerby's style related somewhat to English musical traditions and sometimes struck native Italians as "cold," "Leo Sowerby is thoroughly American, and, despite the allegation of having been influenced by the newer French composer[s], his music could have been written by no one but an American."[28]

Back in Chicago, Maurice Rosenfeld reinforced this American consciousness in a 1924 article on *Two American Pieces*, a piano/violin duo tinged with folklike melodies, which had recently won the grand prize in a *Daily News* contest. Specifically referencing Sowerby's earlier comments about the "disgusting" Salzburg repertory, Rosenfeld took this opportunity to situate Sowerby's Americanism against this frame by spotlighting his melodic elegance and expressiveness.

> But of late there is much consequence, refinement and melody in his works, and no doubt his visit to Salzburg, where he represented America, had much to do with the tempering of his own writings. . . . So perhaps hearing this weird, unordered, dissonant music of others has given him a retrospective notion of writing music for music's sake—for the purpose of making it the expression of song, of emotion, and not just for the purpose of showing how clever, how inscrutable, how erratic a composer can be.[29]

*Two American Pieces* was one of two Roman compositions to take direct inspiration from the homeland. The other is one of Sowerby's best-known works, *From the Northland: Impressions of the Lake Superior Country*, a five-movement suite for piano. The third piece he composed while in Rome, *From the Northland* originated from a 1919 trip to the Canadian woods surrounding Lakes Superior and Huron. Like his earlier *Comes Autumn Time*, *From the Northland* combines traditional forms with programmatic depiction, and Sowerby himself supplied the descriptive narrations for each of the five movements. The first movement, "Forest Voices," displays his continued interest in intricate rhythmic manipulation and chromatic enrichment within a tonal framework (D major). Sowerby's narrative conveys a mystical cast: "In the depth of the green, dark forest I hear not a sound, save the faint magic murmur of the great trees, which seem to chant a song, hushed and mysterious, which betimes surges and swells, and lapses again into primeval silence."

The movement opens in a mood of desolation, set by a gently pulsating left-hand eighth-note pattern in 7/8 meter. Atop this foundation a slow, arc-shaped theme unfolds in irregular rhythms, recalling the free rhythm of chant. The theme is repeated an octave higher while repeated motivic interjections, harmonized in various combinations of parallel intervals, evoke the murmuring trees. A second thematic idea appears as the music commences its "surges and swells," a series of repeating accompaniment patterns with chromatically enriched harmonies, rhythmic accelerations, and changing meters. This climaxes with four broad melodic sweeps, cast amid varied statements of the second theme. After this point the swelling recedes as the rhythms decelerate and the second theme makes one last appearance. The first theme then returns alongside a harmonized version of the opening accompaniment pattern, after which the music momentarily emphasizes the tritone A-flat before returning to D major. After a final utterance of the second theme, the first theme melody is then altered using consecutive tritone intervallic ascents, yielding to the "primeval silence" of the final moments.

In the summer of 1923 Antonio Pedrotti, a conductor who became one of Sowerby's close friends, presented a marked-up version of the piano score with suggestions for orchestration. Sowerby quickly adapted the piece based on Pedrotti's suggestions, omitting one movement, and Hanson premiered the revised version on May 24, 1924, at the AAR with the Orchestra of the Augusteo. This version soon made the rounds with American orchestras in Minneapolis, St. Louis, and elsewhere. In Minneapolis, Southworth Alden of the *Minneapolis Daily Star* was especially eager to promote the piece, to the point of co-opting Sowerby's Americanism for his own midwestern context: "[Sowerby's] 'Comes Autumn Time' overture has thrilled me several times in past seasons. And now comes his suite 'From the Northland' which probably tells as good a story of Minnesota scenery as of Michigan which it probably represents."[30]

Another large-scale work of Sowerby's Rome years was the *Ballad of King Estmere* for two pianos and orchestra, inspired by a ballad in Thomas Percy's *Reliques of Ancient English Poetry*. He composed the piece for Guy Maier and Lee Pattison, a renowned piano duo who had commissioned it prior to Sowerby's leaving America. It was premiered at the Augusteo in Rome on April 8, 1923, with Sowerby and Carlo Zecchi as piano soloists, and Maier and Pattison then toured the piece with Leopold Stokowski and the Philadelphia Orchestra. Two Chicago Symphony performances, on February 15–16, 1924, were especially successful according to Eric DeLamarter, who wrote in a letter: "Dear Leo: Your piece was an immense hit—critics, public, and orchestra. Don't tell, but I think it'll be done again this season."[31]

The most ambitious of Sowerby's Rome-period works was a mammoth five-movement work for orchestra, organ, chorus, and soloists, commonly dubbed the *Psalm Symphony* although Sowerby never attached a formal name to the work. The piece bears clear parallels to Gustav Mahler's Symphony No. 8, in terms of both its monumental scope and its textual focus on redemption through divine love. Composed between May 12, 1923, and April 19, 1924, this oratorio/symphony sets a variety of lengthy Psalm texts, though nearly half the text is nonscriptural and the source of that material remains unknown.[32] Ronald Huntington has observed that Sowerby was likely inspired to compose this work by his patron Coolidge, who had visited the AAR in April 1923. He may have drawn further inspiration from the Three Choirs Festival in Gloucester, which he attended in summer 1922 and which provided his first exposure to massive choral-orchestral works of this sort. It is probable that Sowerby never expected the work to be performed, and indeed it remains unpublished and unrecorded to this day, although a May 4, 2021, performance of excerpts at the University of Kansas has brought it to recent light.[33]

## Jazz and Folk

After three years in Europe, Sowerby returned stateside in September 1924. His first port of call was the Berkshire Festival in Massachusetts, where on September 18 he performed his Sonata for Violoncello and Piano (1921) with violinist Hans Kindler. Heading after this point to Chicago, Sowerby resumed his position as DeLamarter's assistant at Fourth Presbyterian, playing organ for afternoon and evening services, and he also took up residence in DeLamarter's home on Barry Avenue. He additionally joined the faculty at the American Conservatory, teaching music theory and history. Here he developed some highly productive professional relationships, especially with violist and lifelong friend Stella Roberts (whom he dubbed "the one person who knew more about more music than I do"), though he clashed with the conservatory's organ teacher, Wilhelm Middelschulte.

Among Sowerby's most noteworthy projects of the immediate post-Rome era are two pieces centered on jazz. Fueled by the Great Migration and led by figures such as King Oliver and Jelly Roll Morton, jazz had firmly taken hold in Chicago across the 1920s. One of the era's most popular bandleaders was Paul Whiteman, a classical violist by training whose written-out symphonic arrangements and expansive orchestral forces led many to proclaim him the "King of Jazz." Sowerby met Whiteman shortly after returning to Chicago, and Whiteman subsequently commissioned him to write a piece for his orchestra. Sowerby responded with *Synconata*, a piece in sonata form that he termed a "jazz poem." Whiteman premiered the work on December 28, 1924, at New York's Metropolitan Opera House and then took it on tour in spring 1925, performing it some eighty times overall.

By this time Sowerby had become an avowed jazz proponent, valuing especially its potential to help define the "American" in music. In a December 2, 1924, letter to Otto H. Kahn, a powerful New York arts patron, Sowerby's student and close friend Lorry Northrup sought to bring Sowerby to Kahn's attention as "a young American composer of unmistakable genius, whose conviction of the same vital qualities in 'jazz' is plainly discernible in all his great orchestral works." Observing that Kahn was himself also intrigued by jazz, Northrup predicted that "familiarity with Mr. Sowerby's compositions will convince you that he is destined to lead serious American composers in the work of creating a distinctively American musical art."[34]

In another letter three weeks later, this time to the editor of the *New York Telegram and Evening Mail*, Northrup sought to promote *Synconata* by emphasizing the monumentality of a "classical" composer like Sowerby adopting jazz idioms: "When a man like Mr. Sowerby turns his talents from the field of conventional composition to the preparation of a special selection for a 'jass' band, the result should be interesting, and for a purpose." Northrup cites a quotation from Sowerby himself, which leaves no doubt about jazz's centrality to questions of national musical identity: "It is my deep conviction that 'jazz' is to provide the source of an American school of music that should be as distinctive, permanent, and genuine as are the German, French, or Italian idioms."[35]

If jazz elements add a certain color to some of Sowerby's earlier concert works, *Synconata* now pushes these elements front and center. As Northrup describes in his *Telegram and Evening Mail* letter, jazz infuses everything from the piece's hybrid instrumentation (violins, banjo, pianos, drums, trumpets, French horns, trombone, tuba/string bass, reeds) to its syncopated rhythms and colorful harmonies, even as the piece also retains the trappings of classical sonata form. Sowerby himself remarked that he viewed the piece as "serious music, but not solemn. I hope it is American—tuneful and lively."[36] Swinging rhythms and syncopation predominate across the ten-minute piece, infused with Sowerby's trademark complex harmonies, permeated with "blue notes," extended chords, and elements of modality. The songlike main theme is lively and catchy, infused with repeating motives that give it a distinctive popular edge. Yet aspects of Sowerby's "concert" style persist in terms of large-scale sectional planning, frequent tempo shifts, textural variety, and sweeping melodic gestures.

*Synconata*'s success prompted Whiteman to request another, larger work for the orchestra. To prepare for this Sowerby traveled with the Whiteman Orchestra for several weeks, learning about each musician's individual capabilities and further absorbing the symphonic jazz idiom. This second work, titled *Monotony*, was composed between June 4 and August 15, 1925, and was dedicated to both Northrup and Arthur Kudner, an advertising executive. Its four movements, lasting about forty minutes total, each contain a series of fanciful titles: (1) "Nights Out":

The Wary Babbitt—The Invitation Out—The Ineffectual Protest—Table d'hote;
Aisle Seats—The Snore Relapse—Snatched Home; (2) "Fridays at Five": Chat-
ter—Pekoe and Pique—Neurasthenics—Choice Bits—The Scandal—test-t-t-t-t;
(3) "Sermons": Voluntary—Warming Up—The Offertory—Full-Cry—Working
to Beat Hell; (4) "Critics": Enter Chairmen of the Bored—The Sycophant—The
Sentimentalist—The Fussbudget—The Ancient Mariner—The Sophisticate—
Orpheus at Bay.

Whiteman's orchestra performed *Monotony* in Kalamazoo, Michigan, in early
October, prior to a formal premiere on October 11, 1925, in Chicago's Auditorium
Theater, complete with staging and costumes. A *Chicago Daily Journal* review of
this performance paints the scene: "The curtain opens on a moribund purplish
and sulphurous stage setting. A ten-foot metronome stands before the orchestra,
a giant finger waving with insane regularity back and forth. . . . The musicians
were attired in blue smocks and helmets crowned by cogged wheels in harmony
with the scenery, which was all of colored wheels—a gigantic motionless machine,
as amorphous as the symbolic composition which may herald the advent of the
long-awaited new American music."[37]

*Synconata* and *Monotony* are Sowerby's only two discrete jazz compositions.
Though he clearly supported jazz as a viable idiom, and by his own admission he
enjoyed spending time with Whiteman's orchestra, Sowerby never envisioned a
career in this realm.[38] Instead, his professional inclinations began to tilt toward
the church. Along with his existing position at Fourth Presbyterian, he filled in
for six weeks in November-December 1925 at Saint James Episcopal Church
(later Saint James Cathedral) following the sudden departure of its organist and
choirmaster, John W. Norton, who suffered a nervous breakdown and later committed suicide. In April 1926 he added a position as organist and music director
of First Methodist Church in Evanston, though he remained there only thirteen
months (which he termed "thirteen months too many," dissatisfied with having
only a solo quartet rather than choir and never truly connecting with the community).[39] Two notable choral anthems from 1926, "When the Lord Turned Again"
and "Oh Dearest Jesus," also marked a return to sacred choral composition after
several years' absence.

Two other large-scale concert projects, meanwhile, also resonated with sacred
imagery. First was *The Vision of Sir Launfal* (1925), a thirty-minute cantata for ATB
soloists, chorus, orchestra, and optional children's chorus. This work is based on
excerpts from James Russell Lowell's poem of the same name, about a medieval
knight searching for the Holy Grail. The second, in response to a National Association of Organists commission, was a *Medieval Poem* for organ and orchestra,

inspired by the text "Let all mortal flesh keep silence" from the ancient Liturgy of Saint James. Sowerby sketched this work January 9–19, 1926, completed it the following month, and dedicated it to his friend Howard Hanson. It premiered on April 20, 1926, in Chicago's Kimball Hall, with members of the Chicago Symphony conducted by DeLamarter along with Rollo Maitland as organist. In his program notes, Sowerby observed he "has endeavored to interpret the atmosphere of mystery which pervade the poem by translating into tone something of the vision of the heavenly pageant which St. James or any devout soul might have imagined."[40] The piece's form—a set of variations in which the unaltered main theme appears only toward the end—recalls d'Indy's *Istar Variations* and demonstrates Sowerby's continued attention to French models.[41]

Across all these developments, Sowerby continued to embrace the folk materials that had first captivated him the previous decade. Among his direct folk-inspired works of the 1920s are "Old English Songs" for voice, arranged with various accompaniments (1922–23); an arrangement of "Money Musk," a "country tune for piano" which he also orchestrated (1924); a cello-piano arrangement of "Folk-Tunes from Somerset: The Cuckoo" (1927); and a setting of "Pop Goes the Weasel" for woodwind quintet (1927). Though never going as far as Grainger or Bartók in terms of collecting original folk melodies, Sowerby highly valued folk idioms as a cornerstone for future compositional constructions and for carving out distinctive American styles.

Of course, Sowerby was hardly the first American to engage with this material. As Douglas Shadle has described, many nineteenth-century figures believed that folk song would become central to American musical style, notwithstanding the nation's heterogeneity and despite these figures' blindness to "the realities of segregation, disenfranchisement, brutalization, and relocation of nonwhite racial and ethnic groups."[42] The experience of Antonín Dvořák as director of New York's National Conservatory of Music, his efforts to uncover "American" music, and the premiere of his Symphony No. 9 all brought questions of folk music (and especially "negro melodies") into sharp relief.[43]

Sowerby, for his part, viewed folk music as a guiding force for musical modernism, a means of severing the shackles of Germanic tradition and developing a more "authentic" voice. In a 1927 article for *The Musical Scrap Book Magazine* entitled, "The Folk-Element—The Vitalizer of Modern Music," he argues that most of the truly significant innovations in modern music now spring from outside Germany, the very heritage from which he and so many other American composers had been weaned.[44] Like many other modernists he directly rejects the "three B's" and the hegemonic German Romantic tradition, citing in particular the Great

War as a "rude awakening" and the "rather natural desire to avoid contact with all things Teutonic."[45]

In place of this tradition, folk elements now provide the "new" content of modern music. To argue this point Sowerby cites a range of symphonic music across various European cultures, claiming that these traditions have been revitalized through a return to native materials. But his goal is not simply to revive past stylistic techniques, and in fact he distinctly critiques Stravinsky for his turn toward neoclassicism, even as he also hails the composer's other music as "epoch-making."[46] Sowerby's ideal is rather to connect with the timeless, native tradition of one's people, which in his view helps composers become more truly themselves. Yet it should also be acknowledged that such proclamations have not necessarily aged well; Beth Levy, for instance, has cited "a squarely Romantic rhetoric of race and sincerity" in such Sowerby statements as "The world admires, not the eclectic; who can adopt anyone's language, but the man who speaks that which is deep within his own soul, and which reflects the imaginings and the very being of his race."[47]

In advocating for this folk element, Sowerby renounces several contemporary Germanic composers who are nowadays identified as core modernists. About Schoenberg for instance, he observes that the composer's "mathematical mind" has produced atonal music that is "striking" but "has little beauty as music, is hard and dry, and when all is said, boresome."[48] Richard Strauss, meanwhile, "has descended to the repetition of commonplace platitudes" in Sowerby's view (a presumable reference to his shift from the more modernist idioms of *Salome* and *Elektra* to the more anachronistic elements of works like *Der Rosenkavalier*). Other composers, in contrast, "have found the way in steeping themselves in the native, uncultured or even primitive music of their own people. They are thus better able to express the emotions and aspirations of their people, and in so doing, they become more truly themselves."[49]

## Chicago and American Music

In many ways, Chicago offered a uniquely hospitable environment for Sowerby to develop his national consciousness. CSO conductor Frederick Stock was unabashedly supportive of American composers across the 1920s and 1930s, even more so than many of his peers. As Dena Epstein has documented, Stock perpetuated and even expanded upon the practice of his mentor, CSO founder Theodore Thomas, in terms of regularly programming American works.[50] By 1930 Stock was boldly proclaiming that, "for the first time in history, Americans are writing better symphonic music than Europeans"—citing Sowerby by name as one of several noteworthy examples.[51] Stock and Sowerby ultimately developed a long and profitable professional relationship, and they share some other notable parallels as well: besides their mutual support of American music, both were unassuming personalities who enjoyed great success during their lifetimes but have since suffered neglect. Further confirming Chicago's centrality for American symphonic activity, Howard Hanson revealed in a 1938 report for the Music Teachers' National Association that, over the preceding twenty years, the CSO led all American orchestras in premiering works by American composers (272 separate compositions, as opposed to 233 for Boston, 160 for New York, and 152 for Philadelphia).[52]

Sowerby's prominence during this period also invites comparison with another major Chicago-based composer, John Alden Carpenter. Though their lives occupied somewhat different spheres (Carpenter was a businessman when not composing, while Sowerby ultimately found a home in the church), they shared many common features, on paper at least: French-influenced impressionism, a focus on "American" idioms, an interest in jazz, membership in the Cliff Dwellers, as well as the ardent support of Stock. Carpenter helped sponsor multiple Sowerby concerts in the early part of his career, and Sowerby in turn expressed praise for Carpenter's music. In 1921, for instance, Sowerby commended both Carpenter's symphony *Sermons in Stones* and his Piano Concertino as "distinctively American . . . by virtue of their big sweep, their vigor, their lack of sentimentality, affectation and diffuseness."[53]

At the same time, Carpenter's modernism was not something Sowerby himself sought to emulate. The flamboyant jazz-inspired ballet *Skyscrapers* (1926), for instance, conveys an edgier aesthetic than either Sowerby's *Synconata* or *Monotony*, while the gloomy darkness of Carpenter's Walt Whitman—inspired tone poem *Sea Drift* (1933) is far removed from Sowerby's more picturesque *From the Northland*. There is also little direct evidence of a close personal relationship between the two. Howard Pollack suggests that a 1926 disagreement over whether Felix Lamond should be replaced as head of the Music Department at the Academy of Rome may have cooled their friendship, though a letter survives from 1946 in which Carpenter warmly congratulates Sowerby on winning the Pulitzer Prize ("I was delighted to read this morning of the signal honor [so richly deserved!] which has been conferred on you by the Pulitzer Committee.").[54]

Importantly as well, the Chicago scene was in flux during this period in terms of racial and gender dynamics. As Samantha Ege has observed, Florence Price and Theodora Sturkow Ryder both carved out highly successful careers in Chicago while negotiating a battery of gender-, race-, and class-based hurdles.[55] Price, whose Symphony No. 1 in E Minor the CSO premiered in 1933, was hailed as "the first woman of color to produce a symphony and have it featured by one of the great orchestras of the country," a testament to both Chicago's standing and the Black individuals and communities that laid the foundation for her success.[56] Both Price and Sturkow Ryder held nationalist leanings in terms of advocating for American voices, and several of their works resonate with Chicago connections, from pictorial evocations of actual Chicago locales (seen in Sturkow Ryder's piano *Fantasie Pastoral* and operetta *Stockyards Sally*, as well as Price's *Fantasie Negre* for piano solo and orchestral poem *Chicago*) to larger resonances of tradition, identity, assimilation, and urbanization.

Sowerby's young adulthood can be seen in many ways as an open landscape, full of promise and opportunity. From his success as both pianist and composer with major orchestras and chamber ensembles, to his broadening international exposure and his ever-growing standing among Chicago musical society figures, Sowerby was increasingly perceived as an important new voice on the American scene. His willingness to speak frankly and critically about modernist trends bears witness to a potent desire to impact the national conversation on American music, even if his hostility to outsize experimentalism and his emphasis on traditional forms and genres ultimately proved a detriment to his legacy.

In theory, Sowerby's interest in jazz and folk idioms might have served as nodes of connection to other composers as well, such as Aaron Copland, George Gershwin, and Charles Ives. The reality, however, is that Sowerby's association with these figures never moved beyond the incidental. He displayed no special inclination to cultivate the more "urbane" sensibilities often found among New York–based composers; the burlesque qualities of a piece like Copland's *Music for the Theatre* are far removed from Sowerby's more classically oriented *Synconata*. These two pieces in fact serve as a useful metonym for the growing gap between East Coast versus midwestern compositional outlooks. As Oja has observed, New York emerged during the 1920s as a nexus for modernist composers, in which increasingly varied notions of modernism coexisted with the rise of professional networks that strove particularly toward an internationalist impulse—"not a time of cultural isolationism but rather of reaching out as boldly and ecumenically as possible."[57] Areas like Chicago, in contrast, were sometimes stereotyped as being more provincial in focus. The famed Boston music critic Henry Taylor Parker revealed such prejudices in a March 12, 1932, review of Sowerby's *Prairie* (a piece addressed more fully in chapter 3) when it was presented by Serge Koussevitzky and the Boston Symphony Orchestra.



To be fair, Parker asserts in this same review the necessity of becoming familiar with these "provincial" midwesterners ("Michigan and Illinois, the lake-country of the North, are part of these United States no less than New York or New England. They should have and are gaining spokesmen in the arts. Again Mr. Sowerby is one."). Even so, it is easy to read a sense of superiority and condescension into Parker's laudatory comments about Koussevitzky's decision to program the work: "Though Mr. Sowerby's orchestral poem fell below expectation, the production of it for the first time in the East was creditable to the conductor. . . . Now Dr. Koussevitzky, as he grows in knowledge of this America of ours, is broad-minded enough to understand these regional conditions, to act accordingly."

Sowerby's alignment with "the folk element" may have also put him into conflict with certain leading Americans. The New York critic Paul Rosenfeld, who enjoyed almost cultlike status in the 1920s for his authoritative insights on music and other arts, largely rejected the folk, jazz, and other vernacular elements that Sowerby emphasized. Known for high-minded aesthetic philosophies as well as circuitous prose, Rosenfeld argued for a socially connected American music that expressed the spirit of its age, while also celebrating the individual genius in an almost mystical fashion. Such music was often virile or even barbaric, in contrast to the "escapist" mentality he perceived in the jazz and popular worlds. And however much Sowerby could provoke audiences with his chromatically tinged sonorities, pieces like *Carillon* and *From the Northland* can scarcely be called "barbaric" no matter where the listener comes from.

Though a powerful advocate for many American composers, Rosenfeld was decidedly circumspect toward Sowerby. This is evidenced for instance by a December 1924 review published in *The Dial*, where Rosenfeld dismisses Sowerby for his "heavy-handed musical rhetoric" and snidely declares, "The Music of Mr Leo Sowerby, it is not unknown, is not precisely full of merit. The Time Spirit has cruelly neglected making his home in this serious young man."[59] Rosenfeld's opinions probably had a damaging effect on Sowerby's later career prospects; he was known, for instance, to hold sway with Koussevitzky and other figures associated with the Tanglewood Festival, and it is notable that Koussevitzky, despite his long-term support of Sowerby, never performed his music at Tanglewood.

Though Sowerby's concerns with modernism and American music extended through his career, his conception of these elements ultimately traversed a quite different path from most of his peers. If elements of jazz, folk, and chromaticism are never completely abandoned in Sowerby's music, they would be dramatically reconceived in the next stage of his career, within a new and somewhat surprising environment—choral and organ music for the church.

# The Church Ascendant

## *Chicago and a More "Balanced" Composer (1927–40)*

**IN THE EARLY TWENTIETH CENTURY,** American church music was in a somewhat precarious state. As early as 1902, the scholar Edward Dickinson observed that "no new forms or methods have arisen on this side of the Atlantic. The styles of composition and the systems of practice which have existed among us have simply been transferred from the older countries across the sea. Every form of church music known in Europe flourishes in America, but there is no native school of religious music, just as there is no American school of secular music."[1] Later nineteenth-century trends such as the rise of the professional symphony, the establishment of music conservatories, and increasing American interest in European developments had all hampered interest in such music among composers, musicians, and even the public at large.[2] A sharply worded editorial by Paul Henry Lang, published in 1945 for the *Musical Quarterly*, bemoaned the "almost complete stagnation of what was once—and not very long ago—one of the great glories of the art of music: the *ars sacra*."[3]

To be sure, the landscape was not entirely bleak. The American Guild of Organists, founded in 1896, worked to uphold high standards for organ performance, taking inspiration from the English College of Organists and, more generally, from the Oxford Movement's emphasis on higher-quality music for the church.[4] Episcopal choir schools and men-and-boys choirs were also fairly widespread, though they would suffer declines in the later twentieth century. Certain composers as well, including George Whitefield Chadwick and Horatio Parker, were crafting sacred works with considerable artistry. At the same time, many other composers gave church repertory only passing attention, producing scaled-down works to appeal to congregational tastes. Particularly outside the Episcopal realm, choral church repertory between 1900 and 1930 was typically modest in scope, as congregations subsisted on a diet of hymns, simple vernacular pieces, and music either by older composers such as Handel and Mendelssohn or new works patterned on older models.[5]

Against this background, Sowerby's emergence in the late 1920s as a serious sacred composer is all the more dramatic. In some respects he was the beneficiary of good timing, as signs of renewal were already on the horizon (evidenced for instance by the 1928 founding of a collegiate-level church music program at Union Theological Seminary). Yet Sowerby's own initiative was surely a decisive force. His avid cultivation of new works, commitment to high artistic standards, personal devotion to the Episcopal faith, and increasingly outspoken declarations on church music aesthetics all helped secure his status as a leadership figure. If Sowerby in the earlier 1920s was a mainstay of the American concert tradition, a prominent voice in the debates over America's musical future for whom church music was a secondary (though still important) focus, Sowerby's sacred activities in the post-1927 era initiated a decisive shift in which sacred music occupied a more prominent position.

Through all this, Sowerby did not abandon the concert hall. He maintained a high profile on concert stages throughout the 1930s and early 1940s, and indeed certain of his orchestral works developed quite a devoted following. Especially in Chicago, newspaper critics like Eugene Stinson, Glenn Dillard Gunn, Edward Moore, and Maurice Rosenfeld were broadly familiar with his music and discussed its merits regularly in print, often making comparative judgments between the latest novelty and what had come before. Sowerby also developed important relationships with such leading figures as conductors Serge Koussevitzky, Fritz Reiner, Eugene Ormandy, and the organists E. Power Biggs and Catharine Crozier, while retaining the loyalty of established patrons and mentors like the Chicago Symphony's Frederick Stock. If Sowerby is today remembered primarily for his contributions to sacred music, this is due more to a lopsided reception history than a fair representation of his activities. The years between 1927 and 1940 represented not a wholesale tilting of the scales from secular to sacred, but rather a new balance between the two.

## Saint James and Music for the Episcopal Liturgy

On May 1, 1927, Sowerby began a permanent post as organist and choirmaster of Saint James Church in Chicago (later Saint James Cathedral), adding this position to his academic duties at the American Conservatory. The position was a pivotal moment not only in Sowerby's own career, but in the history of Saint James itself. Over the previous sixty years the church had developed a renowned music tradition, shepherded by a series of illustrious music directors (Dudley Buck, Peter Lutkin, Clarence Dickinson) who had secured high-quality church organs, established concert and recital series, and cultivated a men-and-boys choir of national prominence.[6] Rima Lunin Schultz, in her monograph on the history of Saint James, emphasizes the 1920s in particular as something of a musical boom period, "with music and ceremony so excellent as to rival the grandeur of the late Victorian era."[7] Yet at the time of Sowerby's appointment, the music program had suffered a setback under Percy Darlington de Coster, who had been appointed

Sowerby at the organ of Saint James Church, Chicago (Courtesy of the Special Collections Research Center, Syracuse University Libraries).

organist-choirmaster on New Year's Day 1926 and under whose tenure the boys choir was closed down in favor of a lower-quality mixed choir.[8] Saint James's rector, Reverend Duncan Browne, observed in a March 4, 1927, letter to Sowerby that Chicago churches "are not particularly famed for the quality of their music" but that he felt a kinship to Sowerby in terms of their shared ideals for rendering the services, and that "you not only have it within your power to attain that ideal but also to improve your own reputation, already so excellent, in the world of music."[9]

The zeal with which Sowerby threw himself into this new position can hardly be overstated. Saint James had been eager to bring in fresh blood, and Sowerby responded in full force: reinvigorating the choral program and its new mixed-voice choir, launching a recital series that attracted prominent social patronage, and programming more robust music for the liturgy.[10] Sowerby would later proclaim that one of the most appealing tasks of his new position was "carrying out the rector's one request—to get rid of this tiresome and threadbare music."[11] His initiatives soon attracted public notice, as indicated by Lester W. Groom's commentary in an article for *American Organist* that "Mr. Sowerby's training [of the choir] indicates strength and vitality, the depths of which have not been sounded, and which differs so enjoyably from those conductors whose mainstay is sobbing sentimentality."[12]

Quality repertory, regardless of historical era or stylistic imprint, was Sowerby's top priority from the outset. He addressed the issue publicly as early as 1929, stating, "I try to do the good things of all schools, avoiding all sentimental slush in the form of anthems, and keeping away as far as possible from the threadbare Victorian stuff used in so many churches."[13] The connection to English church music is especially telling; Sowerby had gained exposure to this tradition during his Rome Prize travels, and in his first summer after starting at Saint James he returned to England to further familiarize himself with the liturgy.[14] Later, during another vacation in July 1930, he revisited both the American Academy in Rome and the Three Choirs Festival in Hereford, absorbing repertory while also catching up with old friends.

Sowerby was especially drawn to music from the English cathedral tradition, as indicated by records of choral music sung at Saint James. A list of this repertory, compiled by Raymond Jones, shows a marked emphasis on both early and modern English music. Edward Bairstow, Edward Elgar, Gustav Holst, T. Tertius Noble, Charles Villiers Stanford, Ralph Vaughan Williams, and Charles Wood were all sung frequently, with earlier figures like William Byrd, Orlando Gibbons, Handel, and Henry Purcell also well represented. This repertory coexisted alongside works by various American composers as well as international figures like Palestrina, Bach, Mendelssohn, and Tchaikovsky.[15] Sowerby's high standards extended to the Saint James recital series as well, reflecting a thorough appreciation for historical repertory that put him on the vanguard in terms of American rediscovery of Tudor-era composers.[16]

A year after joining Saint James, Sowerby was confirmed into the Episcopalian church by the bishop of Chicago, Sheldon M. Griswold. Though he had previously been baptized as an infant at Saint Mark's Episcopal Church in Grand Rapids and had sung as a boy soprano in its choir, his early religious exposure was also colored by the Christian Science tradition through the influence of his stepmother, and despite holding several previous organist posts he had not developed a particular spiritual attachment to Christianity.[17] Yet his devotion to the Episcopal church became deeply profound, and it invariably worked its way into his compositions as well. Madeleine Goss has claimed that Sowerby's religious conversion inspired him to develop a more reverent approach to his music, an attitude that is also reflected in Sowerby's later observation that "it is not possible to write satisfactory ecclesiastical music unless praise of God is the purpose."[18]

In later years, Sowerby would become an important statesman on both practical and philosophical matters of church music, advocating for high-quality repertory that matched the artistic standards of secular music. (His writings in these areas will be taken up more fully in chapter 4.) But signs of his perspectives emerged even early into his Saint James appointment. In a 1934 article on Saint James's music for the Diocese of Chicago's monthly magazine, he writes eloquently about the church's rich musical traditions but also stresses the necessity of adapting to current conditions. His own approach to liturgical repertory shows a similar focus, acknowledging Tudor English composers as central but embracing music from all eras, "so long as it be 'churchly' which so much music heard in churches is not." His strong interest in programming music by contemporary composers is leavened by the firm condition that they have "written music definitely for the ritual, and in keeping with the finest traditions of their forefathers." And he concludes the article with something of a call to arms: "We march onward. We are not content merely to accept the traditions of the past, noble as they have been. Not to progress is to stagnate and die. So our music must create new traditions, must reflect our own age, but first and foremost we must remember that music in the church is sung to the Glory of God."[19]

Putting these words into action, Sowerby wasted no time composing his own music for the Saint James liturgy. His first two canticle settings, the Benedictus es, Domine, in B-flat and Jubilate Deo in B-flat, appeared in 1928 and were published that year by the H. W. Gray Company, Sowerby's longtime music publisher. Also dating from this year are several other liturgical settings: Nine Invitatories from the Book of Common Prayer, a setting of the Agnus Dei, and the Sentence from the Burial Service and Kyrie. These were soon followed by additional service music: a Benedicite opera omnia in D Minor from 1929 and a large battery of works from 1930: a mass setting (Office of the Holy Communion in C), another Benedictus in D Minor, the Magnificat and Nunc Dimittis in D, and the Te Deum Laudamus in B-Flat—all published by H. W. Gray. Sowerby could thus claim, by the end of this year, to have composed a full complement of works for morning and evening prayer services as well as the mass. He would continue to revisit these genres over the next twelve years with three more communion services, four more settings of the Benedictus, and one additional setting each of the Te Deum and Jubilate Deo.

Standing alongside these works is an extensive series of anthems, hymns, and large-scale cantatas. Sowerby had been composing choral anthems from 1916 (with his first anthem, "The Lord Bless Thee") through the early 1920s, but he set the genre aside during his first years at Saint James to concentrate on canticles. He returned to it with the 1930 Whitsunday anthem "Like the Beams That from the Sun" and followed this with a steady stream of pieces from 1934 onward. Many of these works were occasional in nature, written for anniversaries or dedications relating to particular religious figures or institutions.[20] A particularly notable example is "Great Is the Lord," a cantata for chorus and orchestra composed for the 1934 celebration of the centennial of Saint James's founding. This was an especially lavish occasion, spanning four separate Sundays and also featuring commissioned works by T. Tertius Noble, William Strickland, Healey Willan, and David McK. Williams.

It perhaps comes as no surprise that Sowerby's choral music can be challenging to perform, placing it out of reach for many church choirs and necessarily limiting its popularity, particularly outside the Episcopal realm.[21] Stylistically, the services, anthems, and hymns employ a musical language in which melodic variety (from short, tuneful figures to lengthy ruminations), harmonic complexity, and textual sensitivity are all paramount. While always retaining a tonal foundation, the intricacies of Sowerby's harmonic language—prominent dissonances, ambiguous tonal centers, abundant extended chords—stand out as his most characteristic feature. Modal qualities, and even elements of jazz and blues, can also be discerned in various works. Sowerby's style has further been viewed as having an "American" flavor; John Ogasapian describes the church music as having "a distinctly American idiom in the manner of a Copland, Ives, or even Gershwin. His materials were traditionally European, but their use was not."[22]

Some of Sowerby's "Americanisms" can be discerned in the opening strains of the Magnificat in D Major. Though D major is clearly established in both the piece's title and the opening organ chord, it is immediately undermined by the choir's meandering melody, incorporating several prominent C-naturals that produce a distinct modal tinge. The C-naturals continue in the succeeding organ line, leading to a succession of accented, chromatically enriched block chords, the last of which would suggest a dominant seventh to D major except for yet another C-natural. As the next phrase proceeds with continued C-naturals, the soprano and tenor melody incorporates both C-naturals and F-naturals near the phrase's

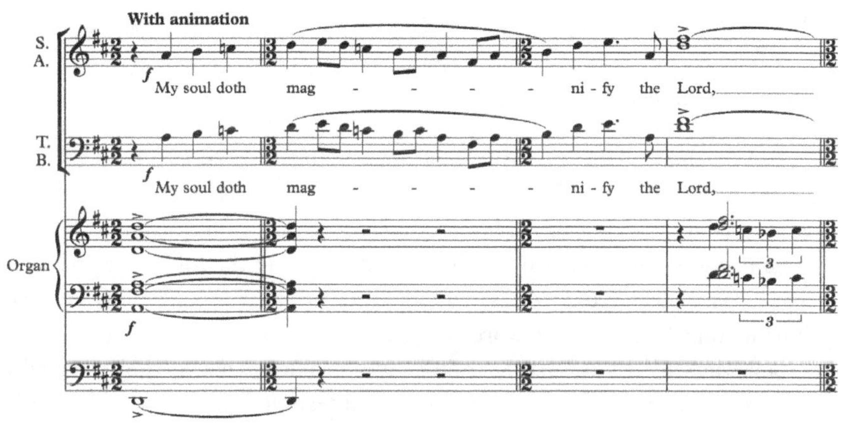

Example 3. Magnificat in D Major, H.200, mm. 1–11 (*continues*)

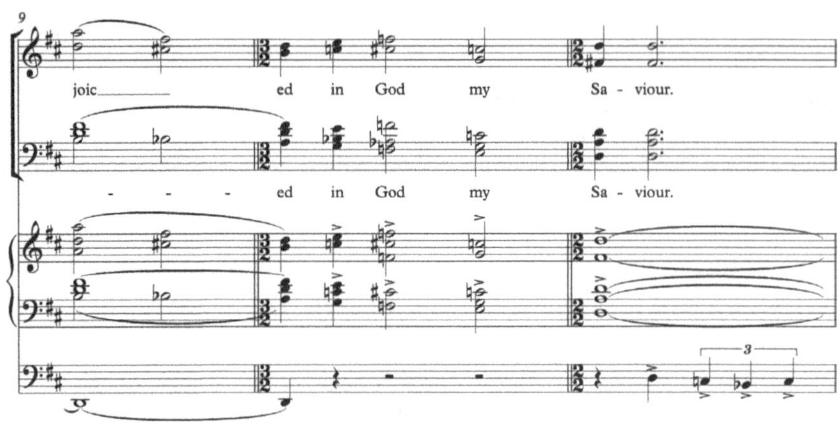


Example 3. *Continued*

conclusion, which might be read as "blue notes" amid the particular tonal context. All these devices occur within a context in which Sowerby is carefully responding to textual concerns. He places a lengthy melisma on the word "magnify," leading to a climactic F-sharp on "Lord"; this then develops in the following phrase as staggered entrances in tenor/bass and soprano/alto lead to arpeggiated leaps that culminate on a high A on the word "rejoice."

Sowerby's ardent focus on liturgical composition was matched by an equally intense approach toward his choir, a mix of volunteers and paid singers. He tightly managed all aspects of the performance milieu, from the rapidly shifting tone colors of his organ music to directing even the spoken "Amens" recited by the choir. He was a taskmaster in rehearsal, closing the doors of the rehearsal room five minutes before the start time and docking the pay of any latecomers. He closely administered his music budget and managed finances to the penny, paying singers with cash out of pocket and individually negotiating their fees. The singers were not especially well paid, as indicated by the fate of Sowerby's favorite singer, the bass John Macdonald (to whom he dedicated his *Three Psalms* for bass and organ [1928]), who eventually left Saint James for a better offer from a Christian Scientist church of $100 per service. Despite all this, Sowerby's micromanagement usually did not faze the singers. "There was always a waiting list to sing with this fine musician," according to his student Robert Rayfield. "He was hard on them too, and exacted the last ounce of effort, with perfection the goal."[23] Personal letters from choir associates from the time confirm this impression, lauding Sowerby's ensemble as being "one of the finest in the area," "precision perfect," and filled with "serious musicians with whom Sowerby did not compromise."[24]

These efforts to professionalize sacred music performance garnered notice well beyond Chicago. The Irish music critic H. L. Morrow, who visited Saint James to witness Sowerby's handiwork at first hand, wrote optimistically in a 1932 *Musical Times* article that Sowerby's ascent might prove a harbinger of better things to come for American church music: "In four years at St. James's, Mr. Sowerby has built up from obscurity a choir that has absorbed the traditional English spirit and style of singing. . . . Much has been said about the standard of American Church music, but here, at all events, is a choir which is certainly winning distinction. The superiority of English choral singing has for so long been taken for granted that it may be surprising to find a nucleus of a serious challenge in our own particular style."[25]

Sowerby's stock began to rise in the Episcopal hierarchy as well. Aside from important relationships with the bishop, clergy, and other members of his immediate circle, his expertise was tapped for the production of a new hymnal for the Episcopal church. In a meeting on October 6–19, 1937, the General Convention of the Episcopal Church had revived the Joint Commission on the Revision of the Hymnal, charged with leading the production of an updated hymnal. Among the commission members was Canon Charles Winfred Douglas, an internationally regarded expert on plainsong. Douglas had headed the production of the earlier

Sowerby with the choir of Saint James Church, Chicago, Easter 1937 (Courtesy of the Special Collections Research Center, Syracuse University Libraries).

1916 hymnal and founded in 1923 the Evergreen Conference School of Music in Colorado, where Sowerby would later become a regular faculty member. When the time came to determine the new hymnal's tunes and harmonizations, Sowerby was seen as an essential authority on the matter, and so he was approached in April 1940 to join the commission.[26]

Musically, the updated 1940 *Hymnal* marked a shift away from Victorian-era tunes and toward the incorporation of plainsong, chorales, and Psalm melodies. The commission emphasized the inclusiveness and universality of its contents, though ironically these same qualities would later be cited as among its shortcomings when the 1940 hymnal was revised in 1982. Sowerby made several contributions to the new volume, including the hymns "Palisades" and "Taylor Hall" and the arrangements "Cradle Hymn," "Twinkling Stars," and "Venite Adoremus," all the latter of which he later also arranged as stand-alone anthems. Canon Douglas's second wife Anne further lauded Sowerby's less visible contributions, such as "his endless patience in helping with the tiresome drudgery of correcting, or improving small snags in harmonization and minor details, for which he would accept no credit or recognition."[27]

## Social and Personal Circumstances

While at Saint James, Sowerby became increasingly settled into a regular social routine. He often took meals at the Cliff Dwellers Club, and a diary of his daily menu over a six-month period shows how heartily he ate there—regular breakfasts, plus full lunches that included a mixture of soups, salads, sandwiches, pasta, and fruit. Steak and potatoes were a clear dinnertime favorite, as he evidently did not like chicken, turkey, or fish except for canned tuna or salmon. This hearty diet, along with a smoking habit that he did not give up until later in life, undoubtedly contributed to his myriad health issues during his final years.[28]

Adding to the situation was Sowerby's penchant for hypochondria, which found him avidly cultivating friends in the medical community.[29] Among these were his student Michael McCabe, who served as an army nurse and became something of a private consultant for Sowerby's health concerns, as well as David Curfman, a doctor who served on the vestry of Saint James Cathedral. Another of his close friends was James Lafayette German, a neurologist at the University of Chicago Medical Center, to whom Sowerby dedicated his Trio for Violin, Violoncello, and Pianoforte (1953). Sowerby and German played chamber music informally and were also united by a shared love for the game of bridge; Sowerby was a competition-caliber bridge player, and enjoyed poker as well.[30]

Sowerby also had certain long-term romantic involvements both prior to and during the Saint James years, including relationships with men from his choir.[31] One relationship was with Clyde Keutzer, a singer and keyboardist who premiered two of Sowerby's compositions: the piano-voice arrangement of his *Old English Songs* (1925), originally scored for two harps, harmonium, and voice; and *Two Songs on Texts by Galsworthy* (1929). Sowerby dedicated three works to Keutzer across several decades: his cantata *A Liturgy of Hope* (1917), the song "Prayer of a Seafarer" (1932), and the choral work Psalm 115 ("Not to Us, O Lord") (1950). Keutzer eventually split with Sowerby and moved to New York, though the two remained on amicable terms, as evidenced by Keutzer's habit of regularly sending Sowerby copies of the *New Yorker* magazine. He ultimately established a varied career in performance, academia, and arts administration, serving as director of the music department at the University of Puget Sound in Seattle, then director of the Hartford School of Music, and later a professor of education at Yeshiva University. Later in life Sowerby's partner was Charles (Chuck) Greene, a bass singer in his choir, a relationship that lasted from 1942 until around 1955. Sowerby dedicated his organ *Rhapsody* (1945) to Greene, and the two were frequent artistic collaborators during this period, including Greene's premiering Sowerby's *Songs of Resignation* (1948) for voice, violin, clarinet, and piano.

On occasion, Sowerby developed romantic interests in his composition students. Ned Rorem, in his memoir *Knowing When to Stop*, describes an incident from 1938 in which he spent a weekend at Sowerby's summer house in Palisades Park, during which Sowerby kissed him following an alcohol-filled evening.[32] A later crush was Kevin Norris, a movie-star handsome organist and composer who was also notorious for heavy drinking. Sowerby dedicated his *Fantasy for Trumpet and Organ* (1961) and the revised version of his Piano Sonata No. 3 in D (1948, rev. 1963) to Norris, while Norris himself dedicated his 1961 Concerto for Organ and Strings to Sowerby.

Unsurprisingly, Sowerby was discreet about his sexual identity. As his own godson Steve Anderson put it, "I knew but I didn't know [about his being gay], but I don't think that anybody thought about it." Because Sowerby organized his life in such a compartmentalized way, it was easy to separate his personal and professional spheres (though he did occasionally blur these lines, for instance by hosting annual choir parties). He also cultivated a rhetoric that pushed aside questions of his personal life, stating repeatedly for instance it would be impossible for him to do what he did as a musician while also being married. Further emblematic of this separation is that Sowerby's longtime residence was an apartment at 5306 Blackstone Avenue, in the Hyde Park neighborhood of south Chicago—a fair distance from Saint James Cathedral, situated north of the city's downtown Loop.

## Music for Organ

Sowerby's installation at Saint James coincided with a fervent recommitment to music for solo organ. After an entire decade (1920–30) in which he composed no such music whatsoever,[33] Sowerby returned to organ composition with alacrity, cultivating a new style which he later termed his "pure organ" period. In contrast to the "orchestral period" of the 1910s, in which rapidly changing tone colors and chromatic harmonies predominate, works of the pure organ period (1930–37) typically feature less sonic variety and are generally more compact and dissonant, with musical ideas that "have grown in depth and intellectuality and are simply and directly expressed."[34] This change was motivated in part by the instruments at his disposal. At Fourth Presbyterian Church, where Sowerby played in 1919–20, the organ was by E. M. Skinner. Though overall quite balanced in tonal families, Skinner's organs placed special emphasis on reed stops that sought to duplicate their particular instruments as closely as possible, which in turn accentuated the organ's ability to produce "orchestral" sounds. The Austin organ at Saint James, however, privileged flutes and strings at the expense of these more colorful reeds.[35] The pure organ phase would in turn be succeeded in 1938 by what Sowerby himself called a "Baroque response" period, characterized by a more linear focus and more direct connections to Baroque genres, though not endeavoring to duplicate the actual sound of historical organs.[36]

Because of Sowerby's lasting reputation as an organ composer par excellence, the lion's share of existing Sowerby studies center on this repertory's stylistic features.[37] Though Sowerby had no single system for composing organ works (or any other works for that matter), certain core themes do emerge.[38] First is the sheer difficulty of the overall repertory; Sowerby's music often makes considerable technical demands, and he saw little need to accommodate performers or to compose scaled-down works for greater public consumption. Second is an enduring regard for traditional genres and techniques: fugue, canon, ostinato, passacaglia, variations, sonata, chorale preludes, and other historical devices all feature regularly among the repertory. Third is a penchant for dissonance and harmonic complexity, though always couched within carefully defined architectural forms. And fourth, Sowerby himself suggested a discrete division between his "concert" and "sacred" organ works, though allowing for some overlap between the two.

Among the concert pieces, the Symphony in G Major (1930–31) is widely regarded as one of Sowerby's finest achievements in any genre. Dedicated to the Canadian organist Lynnwood Farnam, this work exemplifies Sowerby's deep ambitions for the organ as a concert instrument and stands as a landmark of

American large-scale organ composition. Sowerby composed the third-movement Passacaglia first, which Palmer Christian premiered in July 1930 at the National Association of Organists convention in Los Angeles. This single movement was performed several times before Oxford University Press (to which William Walton helped Sowerby gain access) published the fully completed symphony in 1932. Likely performed in Europe thereafter although details remain sketchy, the piece had its American premiere on February 19, 1933, with Harry Benjamin Jepson at Yale University. The symphony soon attracted wide attention as a complex, challenging work—"difficult both to play and to listen to," according to one early reviewer.[39] It was first recorded by E. Power Biggs in 1941 (the first major American organ work to be accorded such sponsorship) and has remained a mainstay of the repertory.

The Organ Symphony has justifiably garnered wide attention for its technical challenges, as well as its blend of forms and techniques from various historical eras.[40] Structurally, this mixture of old and new is evidenced by Sowerby's inverting the classic three-movement tempo scheme to produce a slow-fast-slow pattern. The slow first movement, a sonata form with introduction and coda, showcases a thematic lyricism and expansive scope typical of the later Romantic era. Yet it also contains several modernistic touches, such as alternating 4/2 and 5/2 time signatures and Sowerby's characteristically generous employment of dissonance. Abundant transformations of thematic material, frequent exploration of diverse harmonic areas, and rapidly changing moods are all notable aspects of the movement. The second movement, labeled "Fast and sinister," offers a sharp contrast. Sowerby again upends classical expectations by using rondo form (typically reserved for final movements), but rhythm is perhaps the most notable quality here. Frequent syncopations, ostinato figures, percussive gestures, and a 5/4 meter with pervasive 2+2+1 motives all propel the movement forward and have invoked comparisons to jazz. The rhythmic energy builds as the movement proceeds, culminating in a raucous finale. The final Passacaglia comprises a theme and thirty-three variations. This movement's construction might be viewed in terms of Arnold Schoenberg's notion of developing variation, in that subsequent appearances of the main theme consistently incorporate rhythmic features of earlier iterations.[41] The movement falls into two distinct sections; the first half emphasizes harmonic and rhythmic elements in varying the theme, while the second half exploits various contrapuntal devices (canon, retrograde, inversion, retrograde inversion) in its thematic manipulation.

One of Sowerby's best-known organ pieces, *Pageant* (1931), aptly displays both the composer's careful sense of compositional planning and an inclination to push the boundaries of virtuoso technique. *Pageant* was composed for Fernando Germani, a highly regarded organist at the Basilica of Saint Peter in Rome, with whom Sowerby first became acquainted during his Prix de Rome years. The work is an unabashed showpiece and is especially notorious for its fiendishly difficult pedal part, which Sowerby cultivated specifically to stretch Germani's own legendary pedal abilities. (Upon first receiving the score, Germani reportedly offered Sowerby a sarcastic rejoinder: "Now write me something really difficult!")[42]

*Pageant* has been called "an excellent example of a brilliant show-piece composed with an equal concern with quality."[43] Although the unabashed technical passages instantly command attention, close study of the work reveals Sowerby's deeper interest in subtle manipulations of musical material. The piece is structured as an introduction followed by a theme and four variations, interspersed with a series of interludes and a short coda. As he did in the Passacaglia of his Organ Symphony, Sowerby draws on developing variation in terms of presenting a continuous stream of broadly related motivic material. Elements of this variation occur not simply in transformations of the theme and its harmonic/rhythmic context, but in exploiting differences between the manual and pedal as well.

The introduction presents a heraldic opening theme, whose fanfare-like gestures (along with a tempo indication of "with breadth and sweep") instantly announce both the piece's elevated character and its virtuoso treatment of the pedals. This opening melody germinates from a two-note cell into a type of developing variation, in which subsequent motives elaborate on preceding material in terms of intervallic character, rhythmic patterns, and shifts between pitch registers.

Example 4. *Pageant*, H.205, mm. 1–10

Following this introduction, the main theme appears in the pedal. Rayfield calls this theme "a beautiful example of the Jazz influence," though the melody itself is not especially jazzlike—lyrical, noble, diatonic, rooted in strict four-bar phrases.[44] What Rayfield was more likely referencing is the accompanying harmonic patterns: chromatically enriched chords in the manuals, alternating between offbeat pulses and more flowing passages. Further pedal/manual contrasts are developed in the first variation, now quieter and at a slower tempo; here the manual launches the melody in minor and with sustained accompaniment, before ending back in the major, while the pedal executes vigorous sixteenth-note arpeggios and other rhythmic gestures. For the scherzo-like second variation, the theme migrates between lower and upper registers of the manual amid rapid figurations and chromatic scalar passages, set against pedal points first on G and then B-flat.

In the faster and louder third variation, the theme (now fragmented and chromatically altered) is embedded within an offbeat accompaniment pattern derived from the first variation, while the pedal extends a series of running sixteenth-note figurations derived from the preceding interlude. This leads to the lengthiest of the work's interludes, a virtuoso cadenza interspersed with harmonized fragments of the theme melody. The fourth variation offers the most dramatic textural diversity; the theme begins in the manuals amid accented chords and pedal figurations, but the pedal alone launches the theme's second half with rapid flowing figurations before executing a series of trills and yielding the theme's last phrase to the manual. A final series of pedal flourishes in the coda, against sustained manual chords, brings the piece to a close.

Other organ pieces from the 1930s demonstrate Sowerby's increasing ambition for this instrument. The *Suite for Organ* (1935) anticipates Sowerby's Baroque response period, with four movements (Chorale and Fugue, Fantasy for Flute Stops, Air with Variations, March) that invoke various Baroque forms. *Pageant of Autumn* (1937) also looks backward to Sowerby's earlier oeuvre; the composer himself claimed this piece was like his earlier *Comes Autumn Time*, only longer. *Fanfare* (1938), composed for the new organ at New York's Saint Bartholomew's Episcopal Church, features three sections originally meant to be played on three different sections of the Saint Bartholomew's organ (in the chancel, nave, and dome, respectively).

A crowning achievement in the secular organ realm is the Concerto for Organ and Orchestra (1937–38). Sowerby intended for this to be premiered by organist/conductor Hamilton Harty (who had previously conducted Sowerby's Piano Concerto No. 1) in England, but for unknown reasons Harty was unavailable. In the meantime, Biggs had "quite brashly" requested a large-scale concerto from Sowerby, after doing much to popularize his earlier Symphony in G.[45] Serge Koussevitzky originally wanted Sowerby himself to premiere the work, but lacking the time to gain familiarity with the 1901 George S. Hutchings organ in Symphony Hall, Sowerby proposed that Biggs (who called the Symphony Hall instrument "perfectly awful") be the soloist.

The work premiered on April 22, 1938, with the Boston Symphony Orchestra, to strong reviews. Biggs continued to perform the concerto for several decades afterward, making it one of Sowerby's best-known concert pieces. He was further devoted enough that, after signing a recording contract with Victor Red Seal Records in 1939, he wrote out a five-year plan for future projects that included the Sowerby concerto, adding to this notation "A SUPERB WORK, WHICH SHOULD BE RECORDED AT THE FIRST OPPORTUNITY."[46] (Unfortunately, the recording never took place.) As late as 1963, the concerto was still premiering with a major ensemble like the Philadelphia Orchestra, with Eugene Ormandy conducting it at both Philadelphia's Academy of Music and New York's Lincoln Center. In New York critics like Alan Rich responded positively to the work, but it was audiences who were more dismissive; several patrons reportedly walked out on Sowerby, prompting *New York Times* critic Harold Schonberg to publicly decry their closed-mindedness.[47] Biggs also played the concerto that year with ensembles in Detroit and Wichita, reviving it as late as 1971 at the University of Michigan. Ormandy, for his part, liked the piece enough to follow up by asking Sowerby, "When are you going to write me my symphony?" to which Sowerby would respond with his Symphony No. 5 (1964).[48]

Sowerby's *Toccata* (1939), the first "official" organ piece of the Baroque response period, was completed on November 10, 1939, and manifests many features of this style. Sowerby continually embodies the notion of "response" in this work by closely juxtaposing historical and modern elements. Relentless figurations across the entire work bear out a linear orientation associated with Baroque toccatas, and the overarching ABA form (with bridge and coda) is typical of Sowerby's emphasis on traditional forms. But he responds to these elements with a twentieth-century perspective, rooted in striking harmonies and the development of a small group of thematic gestures with ever-shifting harmonic contexts.

Following a forceful opening chord, the piece launches into a series of restless sixteenth-note arpeggios and other patterns in the swell, set against a contrasting first theme in the great. This stately melody, straightforwardly in C major, contrasts with a focus on A and D in the arpeggios. A short second thematic gesture follows, in quicker rhythms and further reinforcing C major. A near-exact repetition of both these elements with slight harmonic changes leads to an abrupt B-flat chord, launching the third thematic idea: a series of block chords intertwined with further melodic filigree, organized into sequential repeating patterns.

These three themes then make additional appearances, but in each case Sowerby complicates their profiles. When the opening theme appears again it is now transposed to E minor, and the immediately following second gesture vacillates between different keys and modes, rather than reinforcing the established key as it had done before. Two further statements of the third idea follow, both employing untraditional chord progressions and featuring pointed use of dense chromaticism. A fourth gesture then appears near the end of the A section: a stately descending melody in the choir, set against both rapid alternating descending thirds and rising arpeggios in the swell. This material is immediately subjected to repetition and fragmentation, with rapid-fire shifts between choir and swell adding a measure of tone color variety.

Sowerby's penchant for complex sonorities, both in *Toccata* and across his church music, struck his peers as intriguing but also discomfiting. Jim Gray, Sowerby's main publisher, had a penchant for sending him tongue-in-cheek correspondence about the negative reactions that sometimes attended his works. In a note from June 24, 1941, he cites a review from "your friends the Lutherans which isn't so bad as the usual" (i.e., the *Lutheran Journal*), which states that "Although difficult and clashing, unpredictable in voice leading and true to the Sowerby style, this Toccata seems to be the most rational product of the composer's pen that has come to the reviewer's desk. We are looking forward to a composition that does not conform to the world in chaos."[49]

T. Scott Buhrman's review of *Toccata*, from the April 1941 issue of *American Organist*, captures both the clear originality of Sowerby's organ style and the somewhat befuddling effects of his more trenchant harmonic language.

> Dr. Leo Sowerby: TOCCATA, shall we say in C? Let us hear it several times by a competent and sympathetic organist. . . . Player needs a fine technic and a sense of showmanship, for the music must dash along after its business or all is lost. It opens rationally but in a style we must associate with nothing earlier than the present century. The composer does have themes to begin with, musical themes, and he does musical things to them. If dissonances occur, there is reason for them. . . . Nobody objects to ugliness that falls in naturally through dissonances that result from movement of themes, but when dissonances seem to be purposely or carelessly injected merely to create ugliness when the themes are not running that direction themselves, we have a right to be suspicious and ask why.[50]

Sowerby's "Baroque response" sensibility carried over into works beyond the organ repertory. Among the most ambitious of these is *Forsaken of Man* (1939), a large-scale, four-part cantata for choir, soloists, and organ setting the Passion story from the Gospel of Matthew, supplemented with material from the other gospels and original texts for the chorus. The libretto came from Edward Borgers, who originally approached Sowerby in 1935 while a student at the University of Chicago, asking him to review an opera libretto he had written. Sowerby was cool to this particular idea ("I never write opera" was his purported response) but a friendship was nevertheless born, and in 1938 Sowerby suggested that Borgers produce a text for a new Lenten cantata. *Forsaken of Man* was premiered simultaneously on Good Friday 1940 at two Chicago churches, Sowerby's own Saint James Church as well as Hyde Park Methodist Church. It met with broad critical approval and became especially popular at the National Cathedral in Washington, DC, an institution with which Sowerby would later develop a close relationship; here it was sung almost annually for many years and was regarded as "the outstanding modern setting of the Passion narrative."[51] A decade later Borgers and Sowerby would try to make lightning strike twice with another cantata for Christmas, *Christ Reborn* (1950), though this piece failed to achieve the same popularity.

*Forsaken of Man* contains several features particularly associated with J. S. Bach. Like the Bach Passions, Sowerby uses a tenor Evangelist as narrator and a baritone to portray Jesus; most of the other soloists are baritones and basses as well. The choral parts use frequent imitative counterpoint along with more homophonic structures, and the chorus both provides dramatic commentary and participates in the action with its nonscriptural texts, similar to their functions in Bach. Musical distinctions between the roles of the Evangelist and Jesus further reflect Bach's practice of differentiating these characters with different types of recitative. In their very first entrances at the beginning of Part I, for instance, the Evangelist delivers a contoured melody focused on D, with a flowing accompaniment atop a sustained lower pedal. Jesus's entrance, in contrast, uses a narrower melody and thicker chordal sonorities—an accompanied recitative texture reminiscent of the continuo-and-strings accompaniment of Bach's *St. Matthew Passion*.

For all these Baroque references, Sowerby's cantata nonetheless remains rooted in a modern sonic world. Never does Sowerby deliberately imitate Bach's fugues, chorales, or da capo arias; instead, the cantata is most notable for its harmonic complexity and large-scale tonal planning.[52] Of particular interest is a carefully organized tonal scheme in which Sowerby gradually breaks down the cantata's tonal focus, strategically using key signatures (and, toward the work's conclusion, no key signature at all) to symbolize the increased doubt, abandonment, and suffering embedded in the Passion narrative.

## Concert Career

Sowerby's prolific career as a church musician did not restrict his concert activities. Quite to the contrary, he remained very active as a symphonic and chamber composer, and throughout the late 1920s and 1930s his music proliferated in American concert halls, enjoying support from conductors including Koussevitzky, Ormandy, and of course his longtime Chicago Symphony supporter Stock. The CSO performed Sowerby so often that he became, in Francis Crociata's words, the orchestra's "*de facto* composer-in-residence."[53] Sowerby traveled internationally as well, and his music was regularly heard and reviewed in Italy, Germany, and elsewhere. This decade saw the premiere of several large-scale orchestral works, including perhaps his best-known concert piece, *Prairie* (1929–30), along with Passacaglia, Interlude and Fugue for orchestra (1931–32), his second symphony (1927–28), a cello concerto (1935), a second piano concerto (1932), and the tone poem *Theme in Yellow* (1938, based on the Carl Sandburg poem of the same name).

Sowerby reviewing a score with Frederick Stock (Courtesy of the Special Collections Research Center, Syracuse University Libraries).

Public recognition of his achievements also accumulated during this period. In 1930 he was elected an honorary member of the College Bandmasters Association, a nod to his army experience as a bandleader. He was further bestowed an honorary doctor of music degree from the Eastman School of Music in 1934, and he was elected to the American Institute of Arts and Letters in 1935. Sowerby's Eastman accolade was further notable for being the occasion upon which he first met the organist Paul Callaway, who became his student, close friend, and collaborator as organist and choirmaster at National Cathedral in Washington, DC.

No single statement can adequately capture Sowerby's compositional practices during this period. But as with the organ repertory described above, certain traits tend to recur. Although Sowerby did not self-identify as a Neoclassicist, many of his works reference Baroque and Classical models explicitly, either in their overall titles (Passacaglia, Interlude and Fugue; Prelude [1934] for piano, Chaconne for tuba and piano [1936]) or within individual movements. Yet he also embraced more expansive, Romantic-era models of the symphony, concerto, and tone poem, and even sometimes blended these notions together; the Passacaglia, Interlude and Fugue, for example, contains what Sowerby himself called a "romantic" musical conception despite its Classical form.[54] Biggs in particular emphasized this element when he asserted that "[Sowerby's] musical idiom, as we all know, was essentially 'romantic modern.'"[55]

Across all this repertory Sowerby maintained a fundamentally tonal orientation, avoiding the more radical impulses of American contemporaries like Henry Cowell and Edgard Varèse. But Sowerby's tonality is a complex enterprise; the dense chromaticism seen in his church repertory is also heavily present in his concert works, along with such features as ambiguous key areas, modal elements, and jazz influences. Sowerby's concern with "the folk element" persisted as well, as evidenced in such pieces as the *Florida Suite* (1929) for piano, *American Rhapsody* (1933) for band, and "Cumberland Dance" (1937) for violin and piano.

These latter pieces draw upon a range of cultural markers: folk melodies, geography, history, as well as more slippery notions of Americana. Like many of his peers, Sowerby sensed that his own time was ripe for the emergence of a modernist, nationally oriented music. He maintained that a kind of ineffable national spirit would soon emerge, one that transcended cultural and geographical differences. A sense of anticipation can be detected in a February 6, 1935, article from the *Colorado Springs Gazette and Telegraph* (whose headline began with the phrase "Sowerby, Greatest of American Composers"), which reported thusly on Sowerby's mindset:

As mentioned earlier (p. 32), some composers of this time connected nationalism with events related to such areas as history, politics, and commemorations. Sowerby, however, seemed to crave a more metaphysical "American" musical identity. Yet the very complexity of America as a nation made this task particularly challenging. "You must remember that this is vast country," Sowerby goes on to relate in the *Colorado Springs Gazette and Telegraph* article. "It also is a relatively new country, and it will require time before this objective can be achieved, and yet I see its signs already." These signs included increased demand of radio audiences for higher-quality music, heightened interest in concerts featuring American composers, and a more general rise of musical consciousness within the United States.

Alongside these American-themed works, Sowerby continued to pursue traditional Classical genres. Probably the most popular of his abstract symphonic works is the Symphony No. 2 in B Minor, Sowerby's third composition in this genre (preceded by the first symphony and the unpublished *Psalm Symphony*). He composed the first two movements in March-April 1927 and the third in November of that year, the orchestration later completed in spring of 1928. Stock and the Chicago Symphony then premiered the work on March 29–30, 1929, to strong reviews. Andersen, Sowerby's former teacher, especially praised the composer's ability to blend classic structural ideals with novel approaches to melody and timbre: "Here is artistry of form combined with great intensiveness of voice leadings. . . . It is classic, broad and solid, and as magnificent a piece of orchestration as has come to my attention."[57] Edward Moore in the *Chicago Tribune* took particular note of the rousing final movement, "a gorgeous fugue which was at the same time a stirring piece of music. The fact is worth recording because so many modern fugues have turned out to be just fugues. This one became music and was one reason why Mr. Sowerby's presence was demanded on the platform after the performance was over."[58]

Several aspects of this symphony reflect a Neoclassic sensibility. All three movements adopt pre-Romantic movement titles, labeled as "Sonatina," "Recitative," and "Fugue," respectively. The work's relative concision (a typical performance lasts around twenty-five minutes) is a dramatic departure from the gargantuan *Psalm Symphony* of a few years prior, and even the term "sonatina" (rather than "sonata") for the first movement emphasizes its compact nature. Sowerby also privileges wind and brass sonorities at many points, recalling the deemphasis on strings that is a hallmark of Stravinsky's Neoclassical repertory.

Aesthetically as well, qualities of clarity and restraint pervade the work.[59] The first movement, cast in sonata form, presents a first theme in the woodwinds, followed by a short bridge and a second theme featuring the oboe. The development, filled mostly with fragments of the first and second themes, crescendos into a modified recapitulation in which the earlier bridge section is expanded and the second theme omitted. Modernist touches include Sowerby's characteristic dense chromatic chords as well as considerable use of irregular time signatures (alternating 3/8 and 2/4 time signatures in the opening, plus a 5/4 signature for the development section). One of the symphony's most arresting moments occurs at the beginning of the second-movement recitative. A solo horn both opens and closes the movement with a languid melody, with the strings providing a plangent response. Many later interactions feature pairs of wind instruments (clarinet and English horn, flute and trumpet), though the strings also gain prominence. The closing movement employs a strict fugue in which fidelity to historical practice is a clear priority; Sowerby himself claimed that "all the devices of inversion, diminution, stretto etc., are used in due course and in the orthodox places."

While Sowerby was completing the Symphony No. 2, he was also working on another piece that would become one of his main calling cards. The symphonic poem *Prairie* is an evocation of rural America, in the tradition of *Comes Autumn Time*, *Money Musk*, and *From the Northland*. Its inspiration was "Prairie," the first poem from the 1918 collection *Cornhuskers* by Carl Sandburg, whom Sowerby had known since being introduced through the literary editor Fannie Butcher in 1917.[60] A three-time Pulitzer Prize winner whose sprawling interests encompassed poetry, prose, journalism, biography, and folksong, Sandburg was for many *the* quintessential twentieth-century American literary figure. At Sandburg's memorial service in September 1967, President Lyndon B. Johnson arrived unannounced and made a speech praising him as "more than the voice of America, more than the poet of its strength and genius. He was America."[61]

In many respects, Sowerby and Sandburg were two peas in a pod. Both were strongly associated with Chicago; both were enamored of folk music; both cultivated themes from American life; and both were patently concerned with how their art would resonate with the American people. Sowerby had written piano accompaniments to more than twenty songs in Sandburg's enormously popular 1927 folksong anthology *The American Songbag*, and Sandburg included Sowerby in this volume's special acknowledgments, praising his use of "The Irish Washerwoman" in his Cello Concerto and lauding "his ownership of himself, his acceptance of hazards. He is as ready for pioneering and for originality as the new century of which he is a part."

Sandburg goes on in this narrative to address certain modernist tensions of the time, in particular the composer's relationship to common society: "One other definite thing is that [Sowerby] does not prize seclusion to the point where he is out of touch with the People. Not 'the peepul' of the politicians, nor the customers of Tin Pan Alley, but rather The Folks, the common human stream that has counted immensely in the history of music."[62] These comments added fuel to the growing national conflict between eastern and midwestern musical sensibilities, and as Beth Levy observes, they place Sowerby distinctly on the side of a broad-based Americana, distinct from "the cheap eclecticism of the politico-commercial creatures of Washington and New York."[63]

The Sandburg excerpt employed by Sowerby reads as follows:

"Have you ever seen a red sunset drip over one of my cornfields, the shore of night stars, the wave lines of dawn up a wheat valley?

"Have you ever heard my threshing crews yelling in the chaff of a strawpile and the running wheat of the wagonboards, my cornhuskers, my harvest hands hauling crops, singing dreams of women, worlds, horizons?"

To this narrative Sowerby added his own programmatic note, as a guide for the listener: "Imagine being alone in an Illinois cornfield, far enough away from railways, motor cars, telephones, and radios to feel at peace and one with the beauty that is about." In later performances by the Chicago Symphony he further described his aim to interpret the moods of various poetic images (red sunset, shore of night stars, wave lines of dawn, threshing crews) in a continuous flow, but refused to offer more specific analysis and indeed expressed disdain for the kind of specificity sometimes associated with program music.

*Prairie* premiered on August 11, 1929, with Sowerby himself conducting the National High School Orchestra. Howard Hanson, who was in attendance, then published the work under the Eastman School of Music imprint and gave its first major performance on March 11, 1931, with the Detroit Symphony. Other major performances followed with the Chicago Symphony (conducted by Stock), the Cleveland Symphony (conducted by Sowerby himself), and the Philadelphia Orchestra, performing at Carnegie Hall under Ormandy's baton. Koussevitzky had earlier conducted Sowerby's *Comes Autumn Time* in 1931 with the Boston Symphony, but it was *Prairie* that turned him into a Sowerby champion; he would later conduct the world premieres of both Sowerby's Concerto for Organ and Orchestra (April 22, 1938) and Symphony No. 4 (January 7, 1949).

Levy views *Prairie* as a space in which existing qualities of musical landscape painting are both embraced and challenged.[64] Her thoughtful analysis highlights Sowerby's tendency toward melodic ambiguity, as a deliberate obfuscation of how the contrary notions of nature and man are represented (and in contrast to the two discrete melodic types that Burnet Tuthill would associate with Sowerby just a few years later: closely knit rhythmic tunes, reminiscent of popular/folk music; versus a more wandering style with lengthy flow).[65] Her analysis of pastoral topics observes how traditional markers (oboe/woodwind timbres, ostinato/drone patterns, melodic echoes) are complicated by qualities such as chromaticism, inconsistent treatment of repeated patterns, and incomplete gestures. Any conception of innocence in the paradisiacal, pastoral prairie is ultimately betrayed by human elements, from the brass military fanfares that first disrupt this idyll to the invocation of mechanical threshers in the most vigorous section of the piece. The result, in Levy's view, is a piece that illustrates Sowerby's "ambivalence about musical, agricultural, and technological 'progress.'"

This sense of ambivalence might extend to the more broadly programmatic nature of the work, which operates more subtly than in earlier pieces of this ilk. Certain of the poem's images are unmistakably reflected in the music, most notably the fast mechanical repetition of the threshers (further highlighted by Sowerby's tempo marking as "fast, and machine like"), as well as the prominent celeste that accentuates the final section's dream images. A generalized mood of solitude can further be extracted from the pervasive use of slow-moving rhythms, shifting textures, and narrow melodic phrases. But framed against earlier programmatic pieces like *From the Northland*, where images such as "Cascades" and "The Lonely Fiddle-Maker" are clearly depicted through devices like undulating scale/arpeggio passages and open-fifth chords reminiscent of tuning strings, Sowerby's prairie invocation is markedly less proscriptive.

Critical reaction to *Prairie* was sharply divided, along lines spanning both aesthetic and geographical prejudices and highlighting the continuing divisiveness associated with questions of how America ought to be represented musically. In Chicago Glenn Dillard Gunn, a longtime Sowerby advocate, called the piece "music so definitely American in feeling and in manner that it seems to have no connection with the art of Europe, ancient or contemporary. . . . It is my impression that this wide mid-western land touched the imagination of composer and poet alike." For Gunn the ambivalence of Sowerby's portrayal was one of its chief virtues, offering a meditative space similar to what Sowerby himself evoked in his program note; he perceived the piece as "purposely vague in rhythmic impulse, rich, if subdued, in color, both harmonic and orchestral, but unmistakable in mood. One rarely hears music designed to be purely contemplative, and this impression Sowerby achieves except in that division dedicated to the threshing crew."[66] In Minneapolis, James Davies extolled *Prairie* as an embodiment of a more authentic America, one that can be found in interior rather than urban coastal environments. He lauded the composer for "depart[ing] from the error of the ways he was treading in a few years ago" in terms of seeking American music in cabarets and dance halls and finding "deeper reflections, sincere efforts to picture what is familiar to everybody who knows the mid-west, finer and more sustained thought, and a not unsuccessful attempt to put into the orchestral voice the impressions created by a study of the poem mentioned."[67]

East Coast critics perhaps inevitably took a more dismissive attitude, despite praise from certain figures like Samuel L. Laciar in Philadelphia and Lawrence Gilman in New York. Philip Hale, writing in the *Boston Herald*, faulted Sowerby for not living up to expectations of an "American" portrayal of the prairie: "Mr. Sandburg is an American poet who sings of his country. Mr. Sowerby's music might have been written by any foreigner feeling the hush and monotony of the plain near his village. Unfortunately in 'Prairie' there is no suggestion of nationality."[68] *Time* magazine's review of the Carnegie Hall performance played up the geographical tensions inherent in American musical consciousness, while also pointing up certain aesthetic biases involved in classifying a composer or a piece of music as American.

> Impressed though New Yorkers may be with the growth of musical appreciation all over the U.S., they still refuse to be convinced by musical verdicts other than their own. For 15 years Chicago has been aware of Leo Sowerby, the red-haired, bespectacled young man who on Sundays sits soberly gowned in the organ loft at St. James's Cathedral. Chicago recognizes him as one of the most important U.S. composers. But New Yorkers who went to last week's Philadelphia Orchestra concert were not deeply impressed by the fact that Conductor Eugene Ormandy had chosen to play Sowerby's Prairie. Listeners for whom most modern music is synonymous with unfathomable din were asked to imagine themselves alone in an Illinois cornfield far away from railways, motorcars, telephones, and radios.[69]

The unnamed critic goes on to praise Sowerby for his evocation of midwestern farmlands, despite "a few carping critics" who were more inclined to credit Sandburg for the piece's effectiveness. But even with such approval, *Prairie* remained an emblem of a particular type of "America" that certain influential figures found difficult to swallow. And though Sowerby's music continued to flourish in American concert halls for many years after *Prairie*'s premiere, the polarized reactions prompted by this work may have been a harbinger for Sowerby's later concert career, in which his public successes became more scattered.

For the moment, however, Sowerby's connections to the concert world remained strong. Many of his concert works appeared at contemporary music festivals, often at the Eastman School of Music, where his friend and colleague Hanson had become director in 1924. Several pieces embraced traditional genres and forms, and the passacaglia was an especially favored classic technique, featuring prominently in his Organ Symphony and in several keyboard pieces even late in his career. Perhaps the most notable example of this is Passacaglia, Interlude and Fugue, a piano work that Sowerby later orchestrated for Stock and the CSO. Originally announced to premiere during the 1932–33 season, it was ultimately delayed until 1934 and later performed on multiple occasions in the 1950s and 1960s. Sowerby's own program note to this piece illustrates his interest in using older techniques not simply for their own sake, but as a launching pad for creative musical thinking. "While the classic design of the Passacaglia has been adhered to rather strictly, the entire conception of the music is unacademic, and if anything, romantic."

Among other works of this period that extended Sowerby's interest in folk repertories, perhaps the most prominent is the tone poem *Theme in Yellow* (1938), written on commission for the CBS Radio Network's series *Everybody's Music*. Like with the earlier *Prairie*, Sowerby took a Sandburg poem for inspiration (the poem begins, "I spot the hills / With yellow balls in autumn. / I light the prairie cornfields / Orange and tawny gold clusters / And I am called pumpkins.")—but unlike *Prairie*, *Theme in Yellow* made little impact on the concert scene. After its single studio broadcast on July 31, 1938, the original score and parts went missing (an unfortunately regular occurrence with Sowerby's music) and the piece remained unperformed until a 1996 recording for Cedille Records.

Sowerby also made numerous appearances as a conductor, typically leading performances of his own music. In 1929 he served as guest conductor at the National Music Camp at Interlochen, Michigan, conducting his recently composed *Prairie*. In 1933 he returned to his hometown of Grand Rapids, conducting the city's newly established symphony in a slate of his own works including *Money Musk*, *The Irish Washerwoman*, and *Comes Autumn Time*. He conducted another program of his own works with the Colorado Springs Symphony Orchestra in 1935.

One further development of the 1930s was that Sowerby's public performances as a concert keyboardist started to wane. Early in his career he often premiered his own keyboard works, and of course he continued to play organ through his position at Saint James, but he increasingly wrote keyboard pieces with other performers in mind. *Pageant* and the Organ Symphony were written for Fernando Germani and Lynnwood Farnam, respectively (though Farnam passed away before having an opportunity to premiere the work). Biggs in particular developed a long and fruitful relationship with Sowerby, premiering and recording his music and becoming a highly visible advocate.

## Sowerby as Pedagogue

Sowerby was, by all accounts, a beloved teacher. He took very seriously his duties at the American Conservatory, eventually succeeding his mentor Arthur Olaf Andersen as head of the theory and composition department in 1934. Though never fond of administrative details like grading and recordkeeping, Sowerby derived great pleasure from the actual teaching process. He enjoyed the student-teacher relationship and often impressed students with his ability to address their musical problems, as well as his facility on the piano.[70] Biggs went as far as to suggest that "he gave too much time to teaching, but that was his way. Certainly there are countless pupils greatly indebted to him."[71]

His approach to theoretical subjects was traditional in nature, focusing on part writing in harmony and counterpoint classes. As a composition teacher he emphasized colorful harmony, clear structure, and rich orchestration. He further stressed values of neatness, accuracy, and avoiding obvious gestures—qualities clearly evident in many of Sowerby's own works as well.[72] As might be expected, he also brought to his academic teaching the same ideals he brought to the choir chancel: rigorous preparation, a practical mindset, a commitment to musical excellence.

Recollections from former students laud Sowerby for his generosity and humanity, as well as his determination to encourage each student's individual voice rather than demanding conformity to his own (or anybody else's) aesthetic. William Ferris, who studied with Sowerby for five years, once shared an anecdote about the intimidation and artistic self-doubt he experienced upon first hearing a live performance of Igor Stravinsky's *The Rite of Spring*. Sowerby's advice was to "forget about copying Stravinsky or anyone else. You can no more change your style than you can change your face. So you might as well get used to it and learn to use it."[73] Gerald Near, among America's most prominent church music composers, also studied with Sowerby in the later 1950s. He described Sowerby's teaching approach as "one of character and integrity" and that one of the most important lessons Sowerby conveyed was "simply the ability to do the job, rather than just talk about it." Near observed that Sowerby never used his own music pedagogically, though he could have easily done so, and that he was quite open to students cultivating techniques that he himself did not espouse, such as serialism.[74]

One of Sowerby's earlier students at the conservatory was Florence Price, who began her studies there in 1929. Their music was sometimes performed together (for instance at a concert in 1933 at Chicago's Kimball Hall), and Sowerby was an advocate of her career.[75] Another of his most famous students was Ned Rorem, who described himself as "socially warm" with Sowerby even while studying with him as a teenager in 1938. He later dedicated his 1947 *Fantasy and Toccata for Organ* to his former teacher (adding in a handwritten note "For Leo—with much affection, Ned"), and in 1944 he also sent Sowerby a manuscript score of his *Prelude and Adagio* for flute, horn, viola, and organ, which he dedicated to Biggs.

At the same time Rorem's attitudes were sometimes more circumspect, as evidenced by excerpts from his memoirs *Knowing When to Stop*, written in his typically provocative style. Here he portrays Sowerby in a rather provincial light, invoking the same type of "urban versus rural" rhetoric seen in other commentaries related to American musical style.

> Leo Sowerby was, with John Alden Carpenter, the most distinguished composer of the Middle West. . . . Of my parents' generation, a bachelor, reddish complexioned . . . and milky skinned, chain smoker of Fatima cigarettes, unglamorous and nonmysterious, likable with a perpetual worried frown, overweight and wearing rimless glasses, earthy, practical, interested in others even when they were talentless, a stickler for basic training. Sowerby was the first composer I ever knew and the last thing a composer was supposed to resemble. He was a friendly pedagogue.
>
> As to Leo's music, I was shy of it. That he served as organist and choirmaster of Saint James' Church on Rush Street (between two gay bars, though he wouldn't have known), and excelled in sacred music, was stuffy and off-putting. Not until 1943, when I heard Paul Callaway in Washington play the haunting and sinuous Arioso for organ solo . . . and a few years later the cantata on texts of St. Francis, did I realize there was more to Sowerby than academic facility.[76]

Rorem's musical idols came from New York (Aaron Copland, Virgil Thomson), and his comments speak to the palpable distance between Sowerby and the contemporary New York scene. Sowerby, for his part, seldom displayed any effort to promote himself among the East Coast "power elite"—a factor that would facilitate his decline in concert halls after the 1940s (and about which more will be said in chapter 4).

Later in his career, Sowerby took on additional summer teaching duties outside the conservatory. In 1944 he joined the faculty of the Evergreen Conference on Church Music, a summer Episcopalian church music school in Evergreen, Colorado. His wide-ranging duties there included teaching analysis, working directly with student composers, and conducting the conference's choral "Sing" event. He remained at Evergreen for about a decade, until he was invited to join the staff of Camp Wa-Li-Ro, an Episcopal summer camp for boy choristers on an island in Lake Erie near Port Clinton, Ohio. Sowerby maintained his association with Wa-Li-Ro for the rest of his life, generally staying for six weeks during the summer (including one week before and one week after the official four-week camp session). And because he was hired essentially on the strength of his reputation, he could largely set his own professional agenda. This largely consisted of composition, including annual pieces he wrote for the camp choirboys, but involved some conducting as well.

The late 1920s and 1930s were transformational for Sowerby in several respects. His increased devotion to church music, as well as his newly energized personal commitment to the Episcopal faith, sowed the seeds for his later prominence as a church composer, musician, and statesman. One might even connect this new sacred focus with a tempering of certain impulses found in select earlier pieces (e.g., the explicitly jazz-focused *Synconata* and *Monotony*). It was also during this period that Sowerby cemented his status in the American concert hall, where he was widely recognized as among the nation's leading artistic voices.

At the same time, many other aspects of Sowerby's artistry remained more consistent. His stylistic language, broadly speaking, did not undergo any fundamental transformation during this period. With the exception of Sowerby's own commentary regarding the periodization of his organ repertory, it would be difficult to classify his music according to early, middle, or later stylistic periods. A clear reliance on older forms and techniques continued to pervade many works of this era, and Sowerby's reputation for complex harmonies (SowerB!) remained in force. All these elements, in tandem with his continued cultivation of folk idioms, assured that Sowerby remained firmly in the national conversation when it came to the future of American music.

# Secular Decline, Sacred Rise (1940–62)

**HOW DO WE REGARD STYLISTIC CONSISTENCY** across a composer's career? Should the person be admired for remaining faithful to a core sensibility, or criticized for failing to change with the times? For those accustomed to understanding musical figures through frameworks of periodization and stylistic development, the prospect of someone holding firm to a core musical language might provoke suspicions of stagnancy, even if their actual music does not warrant such a label.

The above scenario encapsulates the challenge presented by "later Sowerby" to the modern observer. The roughly two decades encompassed by this chapter are broadly categorized by the extension of traits already associated with him. Professionally, his activities followed similar trajectories from the previous decade in terms of maintaining his service at Saint James, continuing to teach theory and composition at the American Conservatory, and composing both sacred and secular music. Stylistically, his works perpetuate features already associated with the composer—dense chromaticism, motivic repetition, reminiscences of folk melodies, adoption of historical forms and techniques.

One dramatic change during this period, however, is the increasing dichotomy between Sowerby's visibility in the church and concert realms. From the 1940s onward Sowerby became a more regular presence at organ and church music conferences, speaking on everything from practical church matters to philosophical issues of modernism and musical aesthetics. But as his professional and personal worlds increasingly centered on the sacred sphere, this proved a double-edged sword when it came to Sowerby's "art" music. While he continued to produce symphonic and chamber music, his distinct emphasis on church activities led to a growing reputation of the composer as simply a sacred specialist.

Sowerby was hardly the only American of this time to struggle with public perceptions. Figures like Howard Hanson, Roy Harris, William Schuman, and many others all saw their reputations decline in the post–World War II era. Having toiled vigorously to articulate individual conceptions of American concert music, these previously well-known composers now found themselves overshadowed by practitioners of serialism and other experimental trends.

Emily Abrams Ansari has recently argued that the Cold War era upended existing notions of American music, sublimating both the rich variety of the 1930s and a more widely shared sense of patriotism during World War II in favor of a more polarizing emphasis on "exceptionalism"—essentially, the idea of America being an unusually virtuous and admirable nation.[1] This new attitude presented challenges to many composers, who needed to decide whether to jump on the exceptionalist bandwagon or else explore more avant-garde styles.[2] Ansari's study focuses on six particular composers (Hanson, Harris, Schumann, Aaron Copland, Virgil Thomson, and Leonard Bernstein) who, though quite different stylistically, were united by "a commitment to fighting the declining prestige of musical Americanism and addressing its politicization."[3] Catchy labels synthesize the nature of how they adapted stylistically to these politicizing trends: Hanson and Schumann were the "American exceptionalists," Thomson the "'apolitical' opportunist," Harris the "disillusioned nationalist," Copland the "principled brand strategist," Bernstein the "frustrated activist."

Sowerby is not considered in this study, and indeed he is perhaps ill suited to its theoretical framework. Whereas each of Ansari's case study composers engaged in a fundamental reassessment of their musical styles, Sowerby more or less maintained his existing aesthetic course and did not respond directly to postwar political currents. Stephen Buzard, organist and music director at Saint James Cathedral in Chicago and a frequent performer and commentator on Sowerby, frames the issue neatly: "He didn't dabble in atonality. He didn't do serialism. He didn't go with the flow of twentieth-century music in the way that so many other composers did. He stuck with his style, which was very much an outgrowth of the late nineteenth century."[4]

None of this should imply, however, that Sowerby buried his head in the pro-verbial sand. He was certainly quite aware of experimentalist currents, and if he personally was not inclined to dip into these waters, he nevertheless held no ill will toward those who did. Freedom of artistic choice, rather than the promotion of a single stylistic mold, was of supreme importance to his thinking. This attitude was made plain in a *Showcase: Music Clubs Magazine* article from 1960, where he argued that the United States now hosted more musical activity than any other nation and that there was plenty of room for all forms of music. And while "radical music does not appeal to me, I do not berate the people who write in that vein—I only ask that they be sincere rather than trying to make a show of themselves."[5]

Open-minded as Sowerby may have been, his continued devotion to post-Romantic idioms ultimately sounded the death knell to his concert hall repu-tation. This fact has also had lasting consequences in terms of perpetuating an imbalance between the reception of Sowerby's sacred music and his concert hall repertory, a problematic circumstance which in many ways defines the composer to the present day.

## Concert Music and Reputational Challenges

The 1940s were a productive decade for Sowerby as an orchestral composer. Large-scale works of this period included his third (1941) and fourth (composed 1944–47, premiered 1949) symphonies, premiered by Stock and Koussevitzky, respectively; a Concert Overture (1941); large-scale concerted works for viola and organ; a *Fantasy on Hymn Tunes* (1943, premiered 1944 under Sowerby's baton); the cantata *The Canticle of the Sun* (1945); and the *Portrait: Fantasy in Triptych* (1946, conducted by Koussevitzky's nephew Fabien Sevitzky and the Indianapolis Sym-phony). Much of Sowerby's art song repertory dates from this period as well, as do a myriad of piano and chamber works, including a piece he agonized over for fifteen years (the Sonata for Piano No. 3 [1948, revised 1963]), for which three performers separately claimed credit for giving the premiere.[6] Although it is true that Sowerby's secular output dropped conspicuously in the post-1950 era, he nonetheless produced a number of works including a *Concertpiece* for organ and orchestra (1951), *All on a Summer's Day* (1954, for the Louisville Symphony), a suite for piano four hands (1959), and assorted smaller-scale pieces.

Since at least the nineteenth century, American composers have regularly struggled to sustain a lasting reputation in orchestral music. There is not yet a twentieth-century equivalent to Douglas Shadle's multifaceted study of the

nineteenth-century American symphony, but the core issues he raises—historical neglect of American figures, questions of nationalism and "American" style,
problematic German domination of both American orchestral repertory and
the American public imagination—remain relevant to Sowerby's experience.[7]
Nicholas Tawa has identified particularly the window from 1935 to the immediate post–World War II era as a time of exceptional unity in American artistic
thought, during which symphonic music came closer than ever before (or since)
to a unified, accessible aesthetic. Citing what Arthur Schlesinger Jr. called "the
desperate necessity of national cohesion within the framework of shared national
ideals," Tawa argues that Americans produced a bumper crop of outstanding symphonic works that are unjustly neglected in modern times.[8] Like Ansari, Tawa
offers snappy titles to represent various composers' approaches—"the romantic
symphony" (Samuel Barber), "the civil symphony" (John Alden Carpenter), "the
dramatic symphony" (Bernstein), "the knotty symphony" (Roger Sessions), and
the like. Sowerby however is notably absent from this list, just as he was absent
from Ansari's study—an unfortunate omission given the undeniable popularity
of his music during this period.

In light of Tawa's emphasis on national ideals, it is notable that Sowerby
also composed several American-themed pieces during this period. These were
inspired by the United States' entrance into the Second World War and represented his last major public effort to compose music with a distinctively "American" identification. Sowerby was one of eighteen composers commissioned by
Cincinnati Symphony conductor Eugene Goossens to write patriotic pieces for
that orchestra that represented "stirring and significant contributions to the war
effort." His contribution was the *Fanfare for Airmen*, scored for wind band and
composed in late 1942; in a letter to Sowerby dated December 21, 1942, Goossens proclaimed it "splendidly written and beautifully conceived . . . in fact, one of
the best I have so far received."[9] (Among the other commissions, the best known
is Aaron Copland's *Fanfare for the Common Man*.) Other works with nationalist
resonance of this period include *Song for America* (1942) for chorus and orchestra,
based on a text by Norman Rosten and broadcast over radio on the *Bell Telephone
Hour*, as well as a descant to the tune "America" (1942).

Sowerby originally composed his Symphony No. 3 in F-sharp Minor for
Koussevitzky, completing the work on July 30, 1940. Around this same time,
however, Sowerby was contacted by Stock who was seeking a piece to com-
memorate the Chicago Symphony's Golden Jubilee celebration. After inquiring
with Koussevitzky, who allowed the substitution and told Sowerby to just write
his next symphony for him, Sowerby dedicated the work to Stock and the CSO,

which gave the premiere on March 6–7, 1941.[10] A recording survives of a later performance in 1946 by the Chicago Philharmonic, but generally the symphony has languished since its premiere and has never been published.

Stylistically, this symphony displays many of the telltale features of Sowerby's earlier works. Brief, repetitive motives permeate the texture, especially in the first movement, which is dominated by a recurring figure comprising several short gestures, which are broadly similar to each other in character. Certain of this movement's themes convey a folklike impression, notably an initial oboe theme whose sprightly rhythms and melodic formulas have the patina of American folk song. Chromaticism is of course in firm evidence, with pervasive dense chordal structures throughout the symphony. The work is a far cry in many respects from a piece like Howard Hanson's own Symphony No. 3, completed just two years earlier in a mold that is far less chromatic and considerably more "romantic" in character.

In terms of reception, *Musical America* praised the symphony for its "refreshing clarity" and "sturdy and forthright" themes, declaring that it "should rank high in American musical literature" and reporting that "the audience listening to it for the first time seemed especially enthusiastic, recalling Mr. Sowerby many times in approval."[11] Other observers, however, were more skeptical. The composer Remi Gassmann, writing in the journal *Modern Music*, granted that the symphony had "a certain eloquence and impersonal charm" but faulted its pacing and chromaticism, claiming there was "too great a chasm between Sowerby's romanticism and his attempts at formalism."[12] Gassmann was not an unbiased listener; his tastes tended toward the avant-garde, and he later became well known for coproducing the all-electronic soundtrack for Alfred Hitchcock's *The Birds* (1963). Yet his comments provide a foretaste of how Sowerby would increasingly be judged against more experimental standards.

One of Sowerby's most fruitful collaborations during this period was with the organist Biggs, who indeed was probably the single most important figure in keeping Sowerby viable in the concert hall. Biggs commissioned or was otherwise instrumental in launching eight different Sowerby organ works, though ironically he hated the one piece actually dedicated to him (*Canon, Chacony and Fugue* [1951]) and never performed it. In 1941 Biggs suggested that Sowerby compose a work for viola, yielding the *Poem for Viola and Organ*, which he premiered with violist William Primrose on April 5, 1941, in an NBC broadcast. In addition to recording and touring Sowerby repertory, Biggs premiered several other Sowerby works over the next decade, including the Classic Concerto for Organ and String Orchestra (1944, with members of the Boston Symphony), Sonatina for Organ (1944), *Ballade* for English horn and organ (1949), a *Concertpiece for Organ and*

Sowerby with E. Power Biggs, Peggy Biggs, and Eugene Ormandy (Courtesy of the Leo Sowerby Foundation).

*Orchestra* (1952), and *Festival Musick* for organ, brass, and kettledrums (1953). He also recorded the Organ Symphony under the Victor label, which when released in April 1942 marked the first major American organ work to be sponsored by a recording company. Biggs also made a second recording of this piece in 1952, though it was never released.

Another important composition of this period was *The Canticle of the Sun*, a thirty-minute cantata for chorus and orchestra setting a poem by Saint Francis of Assisi, translated to English by the nineteenth-century English poet Matthew Arnold. The text is an exuberant hymn of praise to God for the creatures and elements of the world, which are variously personified as brothers (sun, wind, fire), sisters (moon, water, death), and Mother Earth. Commissioned by the Alice M. Ditson Fund at Columbia University, the cantata premiered on April 16, 1945, at Carnegie Hall with the New York Philharmonic and the Schola Cantorum of New York, part of a benefit concert for Armed Forces Master Records, Inc. It received largely positive press notices, with church-focused composers expressing particular enthusiasm. (Seth Bingham deemed the piece "cataclysmic" and "stunning," while Searle Wright called it "enormous and gorgeous.")[13]

Sowerby's canticle is especially noteworthy for drawing inspiration from wide-ranging historical eras, taking various devices and recasting them within a modern harmonic palette.[14] An overarching ritornello form governs the piece, anchored by an opening forty-eight-measure thematic complex, which is also recalled in the work's final measures. These ritornello sections encompass all the work's purely instrumental passages, as well as choral portions in which the text does *not* reference a brother, sister, or mother image. Those images are instead developed in intervening episodes, where Sowerby sets the texts in highly picturesque fashion. A sudden burst of sound heralds the brightness of the sun; a stark depiction of the nighttime moon features shimmering violins against slow-moving melodies in the flute, clarinet, and bassoon; wispy, fluttering gestures in strings and woodwinds give life to the wind.

A single main theme, presented in the cantata's opening measures, provides the foundation for later ritornello statements (see example 5). A dramatic octave leap on F establishes a firm tonal anchor, joined by sustained notes on this same pitch. The melody then descends through a chromatic, modally tinged series of

Example 5. *The Canticle of the Sun*, H.276, mm. 1–9

steps and leaps, before jumping the octave yet again and proceeding through a second descent. The remainder of the forty-eight-measure introduction presents variations on this initial material, differing in actual pitch content but with similar melodic shapes and rhythmic patterns.

Within this overarching ritornello structure, Sowerby further enlivens the Saint Francis of Assisi text with various contrapuntal and text painting devices. He also includes a heavy dose of chromatic complication, manifested through such techniques as extended chords, nontraditional progressions, and ambiguous spaces between major and minor sonorities. Harmonically, the piece is anchored by F and B as opposing tonal centers. The closing moments of the opening ritornello theme dramatically illustrates this polarity; having begun on F and explored various intermediate sonorities, the entire orchestra comes to a full stop on unison B. After this point, the opening thematic motive is presented in unison and the piece drives to a cadence on a unison F—which itself is preceded by a unison B, rather than the expected dominant C chord.

The monumental scale and textual subject matter of *The Canticle of the Sun* invite questions of where this piece falls along the sacred-secular divide. Though on the surface it might appear to be "sacred music," its secular performance context complicates the issue—particularly for a composer like Sowerby, for whom sacred music was inextricably tied to Christian liturgical worship. Indeed, Sowerby himself regarded his *Canticle* as strictly secular music despite its text, a work intended for pure aesthetic appreciation rather than a vehicle for worship. A second issue that arises is whether the piece might reflect aspects of Sowerby's own spiritual inclinations, as has been considered, for instance, with other semi-sacred works of the period such as Igor Stravinsky's *Symphony of Psalms* (1930) and Samuel Barber's *Prayers of Kierkegaard* (1954). Both these works have been construed as expressions of each composer's own spiritual identity, the extent of which, however, has been subject to some debate.[15] Unlike with these composers, however, there is little evidence that Sowerby conceived of his *Canticle* as any expression of personal spirituality. And as shall soon be seen, Sowerby's other writings on spiritual matters provide a far more direct understanding of where his sentiments lay.

Aside from its musical achievements, *The Canticle of the Sun* also garnered for Sowerby one of the highest accolades of his career, the 1946 Pulitzer Prize for Music. Yet, as with the Symphony No. 3 (and increasingly with other works as well), a successful initial reception did not translate into a lasting presence in the canon. Although Francis Crociata notes the Pulitzer accolade kept Sowerby visible enough to attract some later commissions, *The Canticle of the Sun* has received only about a dozen performances since its premiere, mostly using a condensed version of the orchestral score. And although the practical difficulty of amassing large-scale forces was doubtless a factor in the *Canticle*'s neglect, Sowerby's waning concert reputation was in fact a more chronic condition.

Besides the sheer decline in Sowerby's secular compositional output, at least three other forces can be identified as contributors to his reputational decline. First, and perhaps most importantly, was Sowerby's own disinclination to promote himself in the concert arena. Always modest in temperament, Sowerby was unwilling to put in the necessary legwork to bolster his own reputation. As Biggs observed in 1971, "It is perhaps a pity that throughout the long years of his best orchestral writing, he made no effort to promote his works with conductors and orchestras nor did he choose to be involved in musical politics generally. Some substantial support of managers or press, influential in the whole field of music, could have obtained for Sowerby far greater currency of his works during his most creative years."[16] His former student Gail Quillman later suggested that the composer's enormous workload was a contributing factor: "He was so busy creating and teaching and being a church musician that he really didn't have time to play politics on his own behalf."[17]

One telling example of this reticence relates to his winning the Pulitzer Prize. Sowerby revealed after the prize was awarded that he was entirely unaware of having received the honor until a student mentioned it to him. Even more, Sowerby had not even submitted the composition for Pulitzer consideration—his publishing company, H. W. Gray, had done so on his behalf. (In one of his typically droll telegrams, Jim Gray wrote to Sowerby: "Congratulations on the Pulitzer award. Now you'll be harder to sell than ever.")[18] Sowerby did maintain some influential and important advocates in the concert realm, with people like Koussevitzky, Ormandy, and Biggs supporting his music throughout the 1940s and 1950s. But with the passing of longtime symphonic champion Frederick Stock on October 20, 1942, his most reliable pipeline for orchestral performance was now severed.

An anecdote from a 1952 *Chicago Herald-American* article by Charles Buckley offers another vivid sense of the situation. Prompted by a letter from Sowerby requesting his attendance at an upcoming performance at the Chicago chapter of the International Society for Contemporary Music, Buckley reflected on his own guilt for having forgotten the composer. "In the rush of 'newsworthy' coverage, I had not seen Leo for years. To me, this modest, hard-working gentleman is the musical equivalent of a five-star general. When he speaks, I listen."[19] Having chatted with Sowerby on the phone, Buckley reported that Sowerby's standing with the Chicago Symphony had diminished following Stock's death, to the point that "no one had asked him whether he had anything new to offer"—even though both the Boston Symphony and the San Francisco Symphony had recently performed new pieces of his (the Symphony No. 4 and *Concertpiece for Organ and Orchestra*, respectively). His summary assessment: "Leo Sowerby has almost unequally contrapuntal skill; his knowledge of orchestration is exhaustive. And yet, he's so modest that when we hear from him it's as a member of a committee on behalf of someone else; and the story of his own activities comes out only after questioning."

A second issue involves Sowerby's continued association with Chicago, and his concomitant disinclination to develop systematic connections with New York institutions, where many of the post–World War II era's most provocative modernist trends were being fomented. Sowerby remained committed to furthering his relationship with the Chicago Symphony during this period. In correspondence with Fritz Reiner, who became the CSO's music director in 1953, Sowerby invoked his longstanding association with Stock in requesting that Reiner program some of his more recent repertory, including *Theme in Yellow*, *Portrait: Fantasy in Triptych*, and his Symphony No. 4. Reiner however ended up presenting just one Sowerby work (Passacaglia, Interlude and Fugue) on December 8–9, 1955.

Sowerby was certainly known in various East Coast cities, from his longstanding association with Koussevitzky and the Boston Symphony Orchestra to a fast-growing presence in Washington, DC. Yet many of the prejudices toward midwestern music described in chapter 3, in terms of New York being the cosmopolitan center and areas like Chicago necessarily being more "regional" in focus, continued to hold sway. Certain high-profile conductors like Leopold Stokowski and Dmitry Mitropoulos were also noticeably lukewarm toward Sowerby, though Stokowski did conduct *Comes Autumn Time* in Philadelphia and Mitropoulos conducted the Piano Concerto No. 2 at the Venice Festival of Contemporary Music.[20]

Glenn Dillard Gunn brought these notions front and center in a lengthy 1953 assessment of Sowerby's reputation, penned for the *Washington Times-Herald*:

> How does it happen that an American composer, boasting all possible academic degrees both earned and honorary, a winner of the Prix de Rome and Pulitzer Prize (the last awarded for "Canticle to the Sun"), honored by the country's great orchestras, should still not be a box office hero? This can be explained on several grounds. There is, of course, the initial disadvantage attaching to his origin. There is, further, the fact that most of his successes have been gained in Chicago, a city habitually disregarded by the East and especially by New York.[21]

Finally, a third factor in Sowerby's diminished reputation relates to his compositional peers, who held widely diverging attitudes toward his music. Several of them were quite supportive—particularly figures like Barber, Randall Thompson, and Hanson who, like Sowerby himself, sought to extend various Romantic models through their own, fresh musical idioms. Barber and Sowerby were casual

Sowerby at home, 5306 Blackstone Avenue, Chicago (Courtesy of the Special Collections Research Center, Syracuse University Libraries).

friends, holding attitudes of mutual respect as evidenced by a few pieces of surviving correspondence. In a personal letter from 1954 referencing an upcoming *Prayers of Kierkegaard* performance in Chicago, for instance, Barber proclaimed, "I wish I knew how to write for choir the way you do, damn it; so please come and help me to correct the mistakes!"[22] Another composer, Warren Martin, described Sowerby's style in a 1951 article as superior to many of the twentieth century's biggest names. Martin viewed Sowerby as an outgrowth of the late Romantic and post-Romantic tradition, whose music was distinguished especially by his dissonant harmonies. "But in his work dissonance is not used as spice or excitement (as with Shostakovitch), nor does it depart from the tradition in the direction of a broader concept of tonality (Hindemith), a superimposing of tonalities (Milhaud), or a negation of tonality (disciples of Schönberg); rather it is an individualistic elaboration of tried and true conventional practices."[23]

Hanson, for his part, had of course known Sowerby for decades, ever since their years in Rome. Throughout his own career, Hanson repeatedly programmed Sowerby's music and praised it publicly. As early as 1951, he was citing Sowerby as an example of the difficulties faced by twentieth-century American composers in maintaining their profiles amid changing fashions. In a lecture delivered at the University of Nebraska, for example, he observed,

> The history of the performance of Sowerby's works over the past thirty years is an outstanding example of the capriciousness of public taste. In the third decade of the century there was no American symphonic composer more widely and consistently performed. With the advent of the fourth decade, however, critical taste seemed to turn toward music which was more objective in character and the introspective, almost ascetic cast of much of Sowerby's music was temporarily out of favor. This, I believe, is a passing phase and the best of Sowerby's music will, in my opinion, remain as an important part of American literature.[24]

After Sowerby's death, Hanson further lamented that Sowerby's refusal to become more experimental had resulted in fewer performances of his symphonic works and that this was "a distinct loss to the orchestral repertory. I am sure that in the days ahead his orchestral music will come into its own."[25]

The more experimental figures of the 1940s and 1950s, meanwhile—people like George Perle, Milton Babbitt, and John Cage—simply operated in realms that were foreign to Sowerby, and there is little evidence of any direct engagement among them. Other peers as well had more distant attitudes, which they sometimes proclaimed openly. In a 1936 article for *Modern Music*, "Our Younger Generation—Ten Years Later," a sequel to his 1926 assessment of the American musical scene, Aaron Copland gave an account of Sowerby's talents that emphasized the old-fashioned-ness of both Hanson and Sowerby. "Hanson and Sowerby were well launched even ten years ago [1926]. Their sympathies and natural proclivities make them the heirs of older men such as [Henry Kimball] Hadley and [Arthur] Shepherd. Their facility in writing and their eclectic style produce a kind of palatable music, which cannot be expected to arouse the enthusiasm of the 'elite,' but does serve to fill the role of 'American Music' for broad masses of people."[26] Later, when asked by Francis Crociata about Sowerby, Copland would say only that "he was a very nice man, I'm told he was a very good teacher," without addressing Sowerby's actual music.[27] Virgil Thomson was even more cavalier toward Sowerby, dismissing *The Canticle of the Sun* as second-rate Wagner and Liszt and later crafting his own more intimate setting of this text for voice and piano, a complete contrast aesthetically to Sowerby's setting. Though renowned as an incisive critic, Thomson was also a "bomb-thrower" who has been faulted for sweeping generalizations, blatant promotion of his friends, and simply not understanding many composers or their music (including Wagner).[28] Even so, his attitude is indicative of a growing perception that Sowerby's idioms were out of step with current sensibilities.

Sowerby was less willing to critique individual peers so publicly, but this does not mean that he held no opinions about these figures, or about modern music more generally. In certain contexts—particularly sacred ones—he was actually quite vocal about contemporary music, and there is no shortage of strongly worded directives about modernist values (some of which will be explored later in this chapter). As for his personal image, however, Sowerby simply refused to play the games that occupied so many others. Cecil Smith, writing in 1941 shortly before the premiere of Sowerby's Symphony No. 3, declared outright that "Sowerby does not have much to say about his newest composition," and Sowerby himself is quoted in the same article as finding composers' explanations of their own processes tedious, stating that he is "weary of reading the long dissertations and explanations provided by composers, which often turn out to be mere apologies."[29]

Sowerby certainly did write about his own music at times, as evidenced by both program notes and published articles expressing his ideas about specific compositions or trends. But the tenor of his comments usually remains straightforward and objective, without straying too far into activism or doctrinism. One of his more extended commentaries from 1954, republished four decades later in the program notes to a 1995 program celebrating the centenary of his birth, best sums up his perspective.

> Generally speaking, composers talk too much, particularly about their own works. Many seem to be propagandists instead of composers. My idea always has been to keep clear of cliques, movements, groups and fads. I have no axe to grind in writing music, no propaganda to propagate, nothing to prove. I wish merely to attempt to create art in a craftsmanlike manner, and give out what an inner urge prompts me to give out. No more than that. To unsophisticated musicians my music sounds, as they say, "modern" which means strange, or maybe worse than strange. To sophisticated musicians, it may sound tame or dull, or unexciting, or worse. I am not one to make an evaluation of my music, nor am I one to discuss its spiritual content. It is for the listener to find the message for himself and if he wishes to make it his own by taking it to himself, be assured that the expression is a very sincere one.[30]

## Church Music Composition and Philosophy

In stark contrast to his decreased presence in mainstream artistic currents, Sowerby's status as an authority on church music increased markedly from the 1940s onward. Compositionally his output inclined decisively toward sacred organ and choral music, and by the 1950s this repertory was truly dominating his attention. Dating from this period are certain of Sowerby's most enduring anthems, including Psalm 122 ("I Was Glad When They Said unto Me" [1941]) and the brief but highly evocative "Eternal Light" (1958). These pieces stand alongside a range of other service and anthem settings, as well as large-scale cantatas including *The Throne of God* (1956–57), composed for the fiftieth Anniversary of Washington Cathedral, and *The Ark of the Covenant* (1960), written for the Saint Luke's Episcopal Church Choir in San Francisco. Organ repertory of these years includes well-known works like *Arioso* (1942) and *Rhapsody* (1945), plus an abundance of preludes, fantasies, and other characteristic pieces.

Two works from early in this era offer a snapshot of both Sowerby's stylistic integrity and his facility across wide-ranging idioms. *Arioso*, dedicated to fellow organist and American Conservatory instructor Jack Goode ("J.G. SEMPER IDEM L.S." reads the dedication on the original manuscript), is among Sowerby's more accessible organ pieces. Cast in an ABA form with introduction and coda, the piece embraces typical Sowerby features of harmonic complexity, repetitive gestures, and devotion to older forms. Yet it also bears hints of a more modern jazz influence with abundant extended chords, subtle rhythmic syncopations, melodic "blue notes," and regular intervallic leaps of augmented sevenths and ninths. Both of the work's principal themes are foreshadowed in the opening measures, though the heavy harmonic chromaticism perhaps attracts greater attention. The first theme (see example 6), long and ruminating, invokes the titular arioso style with its songlike lyricism, sweeping breadth, occasional rubato, and clear melody-and-accompaniment texture. Though anchored tonally in A-flat major, several melodic gestures are reminiscent of modal or pentatonic qualities, while the accompaniment patterns move in strict parallel fourth motion.

In the B section, things liven up somewhat. The tempo marking is slightly faster, registrations are shifted, the key signature is removed, and the melody is both more rhapsodic and more rhythmically active—a sharp contrast that would not be out of place in a da capo aria. A short bridge section brings back the A section, now in the left-hand lower octave with a more intricate and repetitive right-hand accompaniment. For the coda the melody moves back into the original upper octave, and the piece then melts into a series of soft closing chords.

A markedly more celebratory piece is Psalm 122, composed for the Rt. Reverend Henry St. George Tucker's installation as presiding bishop of the Episcopal Church at Washington Cathedral and dedicated to him. In England this Psalm text has long been associated with royal coronations, for which musical settings date back to seventeenth-century figures like Thomas Tomkins and Henry Purcell. The

Example 6. *Arioso*, H.260, mm. 15–25

modern standard is the well-known setting by C. Hubert H. Parry, composed in 1902 (and revised in 1911) for the coronations of kings Edward VII and George V, respectively, and habitually used since that time for other English coronations.

Sowerby's anthem, composed within a similar faith tradition for a similar occasion, invites comparison to Parry's setting. His opening gambit certainly seems to borrow a page from the English composer; three distinct ascending organ phrases of similar melodic character are given ever-increasing intensity, just as they are in Parry's own setting. In general, however, Sowerby distinguishes himself especially by cultivating a greater variety of moods. His opening is naturally in a triumphant cast, with its declamatory choral lines, chromatically tinged harmonies, thick textures, and smooth connective passages in the organ. But for the text "Jerusalem is built as a city that is at unity in itself" he switches to fugal mode, as voice parts from bass upward through tenor, alto, and soprano literally "build" the musical texture atop the organ accompaniment (see example 7). The thematic idea itself also suggests the idea of building—the motive ascends mostly stepwise up an octave before descending again, but during each descent the next voice begins the fugue, bringing back the melody's ascending portion and preserving the climb. Later, Sowerby sets the voices up in paired imitation before yielding once again to chordal declamation, the full vocal texture having now been securely built.

Example 7. *Psalm 122*, H.254, mm. 25–33 *(continues)*

Example 7. *Continued*

Throughout the anthem, music-text relations are handled with particular sensitivity. After the exuberant initial Psalm verses, Sowerby shifts the mood dramatically on the phrase "For there is the seat of judgment, even the seat of the house of David." Here an initial forte unison declamation of this text slowly decreases in dynamics; the melody also descends stepwise the distance of a tritone, from D to A-flat, a seeming reflection of the pallor of judgment. The following phrase, "O pray for the peace of Jerusalem," begins with a surprisingly clear sense (by Sowerby standards anyway) of D-flat major, a lyrical and languid soprano line followed by a tenor melody of similar character, set against a brief soprano countermelody. This complex is then repeated in bass and alto, transposed downward to B-flat major, leading to a serene presentation of "Peace be within thy walls, and plenteousness within thy palaces"—a striking contrast from Parry, whose anthem closes with this text and who sets it with unabashed bombast.

Perhaps Sowerby's most arresting textual treatment comes at the anthem's very end. Having cultivated further imitative textures and slowly rebuilt a mood of excitement on "For my brethren and companions' sakes, I will wish thee prosperity," he begins the final phrase "Yea, because of the house of the Lord our God" in similar vigorous fashion, before gradually growing softer on the phrase "I will seek to do thee good." A haunting, sinewy organ melody on the English horn leads to a final, hushed homophonic statement of this phrase—conveying a sense of quiet confidence, as the organ closes the piece with gently ruminating lines and solemn ending chords.

As significant as Sowerby's compositional output was during this period, he was perhaps even more influential as a spokesman on sacred music matters. Especially from the 1950s onward Sowerby truly became a national (and even international) presence, being arguably the most important statesman on American church music. Surprisingly for an organist and organ composer of his stature, Sowerby attended his first American Guild of Organists national convention only in 1952, but thereafter he became a fixture of this scene. He made regular appearances at cathedrals, churches, and sacred music conventions across the country, including Washington, DC (1947, 1949, 1953), Indianapolis (1942, 1947, 1963), San Francisco (1952, 1961), Evergreen, Colorado (1954), Houston (1955, 1958), Ottawa, Canada (1958), Nashville (1959), New York (1963), and London (1957), giving lectures and performing and conducting his own music.

Sowerby was already regarded highly within Episcopal circles by 1940, as evidenced for instance by his being placed on the Joint Commission on Music and the Joint Commission on the Revision of the 1940 *Hymnal.* He maintained a presence in later hymnal revisions as well, authoring the hymns "Berkeley," "Perry," and "Rosedale" as well as an adaptation of the Kyrie. His tireless advocacy of quality music and rigorous standards was certainly appreciated, but importantly these efforts were also viewed as a liability in certain quarters. Carol Doran, in one of several introductory essays from *The Hymnal 1982 Companion* (associated with the Episcopal Church's revised hymnal of that year), observed that the 1982 *Hymnal*'s new focus on "inclusive diversity" stood in contradistinction to earlier, more restrictive approaches—embodied in particular by Sowerby, who was directly faulted for maintaining elevated musical standards that excluded the musically untrained worshipper.[31] In his 1956 essay *Ideals in Church Music* (more on which below), Sowerby had argued that proper church music should be pleasing to both the devout (by bringing them to a devotional state) and to a "musical person" who may not actually be devout themselves; and moreover that it should adopt the same standards as would be expected of concert hall music, eschewing popular/ profane influences in the process.[32] Doran, in contrast, explicitly favored incorporating popular styles into the liturgy. She assailed Sowerby for "discourag[ing] the legitimate participation of many faithful who are neither gifted nor trained in music" and positioned the 1982 *Hymnal* as an aesthetic contrast to 1940's, which had demanded musical uniformity and was guided by a perception that "only the best is good enough for God."[33]

Sowerby receiving citation for outstanding contributions to Episcopal church music, 1960. Left to right: Rev. Thomas R. Gibson (clergy chairman of commission); Rt. Rev. Lauriston L. Scaife (bishop of Diocese of Western New York); Sowerby; Raymond F. Glover (lay chairman of commission, Saint Paul's Cathedral, Buffalo) (Courtesy of the Special Collections Research Center, Syracuse University Libraries).

Formal recognition of Sowerby's contributions also accumulated in his later years. In addition to his Pulitzer honor, on May 25, 1950, Sowerby was awarded a citation from the National Association for American Composers and Conductors for his "untiring efforts and distinguished contribution to the cause of American Music." Another citation, for outstanding contributions to Episcopal church music, came from Bishop Lauriston L. Scaife of the Western New York Diocese at the 1960 fall seminar of the diocese's music commission. In bestowing the award Scaife addressed Sowerby as "the dean of American composers of church music," a well-known phrase that had come to define the composer.

The twenty-fifth anniversary of Sowerby's employment at Saint James, celebrated on April 27, 1952, offered a special opportunity to reflect on his sacred music achievements up to that point. Dozens of testimonials poured in from composers, performers, former students, and clergy, lauding Sowerby's standing as the premier American figure in this realm. Paul Callaway, organist and choirmaster at Washington National Cathedral, proclaimed in a letter to Cathedral Dean Howard S. Kennedy that "it seems to me that this anniversary should be celebrated by the whole church in this country and throughout the world. Dr. Sowerby has done more than any other American to enrich the music of the church."[34] The composer Seth Bingham, meanwhile, remarked in a personal letter to Sowerby that "I hardly need to tell you that thousands of your colleagues including myself regard you as *the* leader in our profession."[35]

Perhaps the most revealing commentary came from Washington Cathedral's Leonard Ellinwood, a musicologist, hymnologist, singer, and deacon whose testimonial offered a glimpse of how the sacred musical environment itself had changed over the years, and how Sowerby had played a decisive role in that change. His comments, contained in a personal letter to Sowerby, are worth quoting in some detail:

> Dear Leo:
>
> We sang your *Forsaken of Man* as usual again on Passion Sunday; on Palm Sunday Paul [Callaway] played your prelude on *King's Majesty*; Easter at Evensong we used your setting of the canticles, repeating the *Nunc dimittis* this afternoon when the Annapolis Naval Academy choir was here and sang a musical service; next Sunday we are using your setting of the *Jubilate Deo*. And so it goes on here month after month, as in an increasing number of choirs throughout the Anglican world.
>
> What a far cry all this is from the situation 25 years ago when I was fresh out of college and you were beginning your years of service at St. James'. Since then your choir, your compositions, and your teaching have played a principal role in effecting the transformation which has taken place in so much of American church music.
>
> No longer do we have to apologize to our fellow musicians for the decadent state of our church music; rather concert goers seek us out in preference to some of the decadence now prevalent in the concert halls.[36]

Across the 1950s and 1960s, Sowerby himself would expound greatly on the "decadent" values described in Ellinwood's letter. In print and in various speeches he engaged with philosophical and theological questions about the role of music in sacred worship, the qualities this music should contain, and to whom should it ultimately be directed. Reviewing these writings systematically, it is not difficult to ascertain the core values Sowerby holds dear: respect for tradition and authority, as well as an understanding that modern music must use contemporary languages while also acknowledging its debts to the past.

Unsurprisingly, Sowerby consistently demanded the highest quality in music for the liturgy, rooted in strict discipline, a tireless work ethic, and uncompromising standards. He developed a reputation among sacred musicians for his heightened intellectualism and rigor, one that was perhaps colored by his continued attention to serious art music, and which led the composer and author Talmage Dean to call him "a prototype of a new professional church musician."[37]

By the same token, Sowerby also held little patience for church music that failed to live up to these standards. A sense of frustration often permeates his rhetoric on the subject, as observed for instance in an article from the December 1958 *Diapason* based on a lecture given for that year's Canadian College of Organists convention in Ottawa.[38]

> The person satisfied with second-rate music is invariably ready to tolerate second-rate performance. A good director knows that it takes real work, hard work on the part of himself and his choir, to achieve a vital and finished performance. Too often we hear indifferent and slovenly readings of trite and commonplace music which is no more or less than an insult to God, to whom, ideally, it is being addressed. It must always be kept in mind that the choir's function, and that of the organist too, is not to entertain those who come to worship but to bring them into closer communion with the Almighty and to present the musical portions of the liturgy as a corporate offering to the Divinity. If the choirmaster would always remember this, he might ofttimes be thoroughly ashamed of the results he achieves; he might then be spurred on to change and improve the situation.[39]

A consistent through-line in Sowerby's thinking on church music is what might be termed an "authoritarian" approach to the subject. For Sowerby, music should glorify divine authorities using the finest possible craft, in a manner that is dignified, sober, and solemn. It should also avoid secular, popular, and sentimental influences that cater to the worshipper's personal edification or entertainment. It should further be performed by trained professionals, serving as musical authorities to produce the finest offerings to God and to elevate the musical tastes of their congregations. Strong centralized musical leadership, and firm adherence to official Episcopal musical and liturgical policies, are also strictly required.

The pamphlet *Ideals in Church Music* began as a paper delivered at various locales in the early 1940s: first in Chicago for the Van Dusen Club in 1941, then in April of that year in Washington, DC, for a church music conference at the National Cathedral, and finally in June 1943 at Saint Bartholomew's Church in New York.[40] It ultimately became an official statement for the Joint Commission on Church Music of the Episcopal Church and was published by Seabury Press in 1956.[41] Though a modest tract of only sixteen pages, this pamphlet was "destined to become required reading for students in many schools of church music," in the words of Dean.[42]

Sowerby makes no bones about his authoritarian perspective in this publication. He asserts it patently in the very first paragraph, where music's connection to a worshipper's personal experience is sublimated in favor of its association with the divine.

> The purpose in music in worship, it has been said, is to strengthen the ideas and feelings that the worshipper already has and to release the mind from life's ordinary activities. This may be true, but it puts the accent in the wrong place—on the worshipper. In reality music in worship is essentially a part of the corporate act of worship and a direct means of approach to God. This music, then, is not primarily a means for edifying, or even inspiring, the worshipper, but is a part of his offering to the Deity.[43]

Sowerby goes on to argue that music must be of a quality suitable for the deity to whom it is addressed. Inferior music should not be tolerated, though in practice it often is. Church music must also be distinctively marked as "sacred," in the sense of omitting "profane and worldly influences," and it should be judged by the same artistic standards as concert hall music.

To support these assertions, Sowerby provides a condensed history of Christian sacred music from plainsong to the present—a review occupying more than half of the pamphlet's total length. His purpose is to offer several models of compositional authority, including plainsong, "Golden Age" Renaissance composers like Josquin de Prez and Palestrina, English Renaissance figures like Tallis and Byrd—and of course Bach, "the supreme universal musician." Classical and Romantic-era composers are generally less authoritative, in the sense of their sacred works following symphonic models and adopting secular influences such as dance and opera.[44]

Regarding modern music, Sowerby argues forcefully that the church must incorporate this repertory into its liturgies, comparing it to other aspects of the worship experience like sermons and physical buildings, which also respond to modern sensibilities. Composers, moreover, should write this music using the idioms of the current day, though they should also be guided by tradition. The need for high-quality modern music is all the greater because of what Sowerby claims is heard far too commonly in church—things like transcriptions of operatic and other light works, banal hymns and chants, and electronic organs. These inferior musical products result from a misunderstanding that church music should appeal to popular tastes rather than divine authority. "The basic idea underlying all the music of the Church is that it is performed as an act of praise, worship, prayer, or thanksgiving directly to God. How wrong, then, is the thought that the people who come to worship must expect that they shall be entertained by the music."[45]

Sowerby followed up on these ideas with two further publications, both issued in 1958. "Composition in Relation to the Church and Allied Fields in America," based on a talk given at the 1957 International Congress of Organists in London, is a sprawling assemblage of thoughts on American church music from both philosophical and practical perspectives.[46] Here Sowerby calls his current era "the age of the Individualist" and says that "in many churches today the theory that the music sung in the services is the means of a direct approach to God would be greeted as a novel one, for the music is too often regarded as a means to soothe, or delight, or excite mere man."[47] The clergy themselves are too often complicit also, neglecting their proper duties through their hostility toward high-quality music.[48]

The second publication, "Church Musician Duties Defined in CCO Lecture," appeared in *The Diapason* as a transcript of a lecture given at the Canadian College of Organists annual convention on August 27, 1958.[49] Though emphasizing the practical obligations of organists and choirmasters, this essay also contains philosophical and theological ideas that reinforce Sowerby's authoritarian ideals. A dramatic illustration of this comes in a remark about how quality music directors/organists might be regarded: "In some of the denominational churches the title 'minister of music' has, in late years, come into increasing use; this, however, has found little favor in the liturgical churches. I might add, in an aside, that the designation 'musical dictator' would be a more accurate one, at least in the places where the best work is done."[50]

Strong musical leadership is a recurring theme in this essay, as a tool for combating the complacency that Sowerby claims is too common among many churches. The reasons for this leadership stance are rooted in themes already seen—God as divine authority, the primacy of quality musical standards over congregational tastes. Sowerby reiterates that "the choir's function, and that of the organist too, is not to entertain those who come to worship but to bring them into closer communion with the Almighty and to present the musical portions of the liturgy as a corporate offering to the Divinity."[51]

Sowerby's philosophy also extends to the issue of conforming to official Episcopal musical and liturgical policies. This is seen especially in "The Compleat Choirmaster," an unpublished manuscript copyrighted in 1961. As in his other writings, Sowerby tackles wide-ranging matters both practical and philosophical, relating to various aspects of the choirmaster's job and the more general use of music in the church. Yet it is here where Sowerby's ideas on conformity are perhaps most emphatically stated. He directly addresses congregational singing, for instance, by framing the 1940 Episcopal *Hymnal* as a matter of corporate authority over individual preference. As a publication prepared by a Joint Commission and appointed by the General Convention, "we should not only *accept* that revision, whether or not we personally approve of it in its entirety, but we should take steps to provide ourselves with that revision at the earliest possible moment."[52]

A unified liturgy is also critical to Sowerby's view. He provides myriad anecdotes about being in some distant locale and experiencing either comfort or frustration when attending a church service, depending on whether or not the customary rubrics were followed. To be sure, a certain degree of leeway and individuality in these can be acceptable; Sowerby is not always a strict absolutist. Yet he puts the matter directly in another quotation from "The Compleat Choirmaster": "Our church is one which believes in, and accepts, authority and discipline. Everyone connected in any way with the conduct of services or worship in our churches should accept this authority and subject himself to this discipline."[53]

Sowerby's viewpoints were in many ways an extension of broader impulses toward musical professionalism from earlier in the twentieth century.[54] The emergence of Anglican-style men-and-boys choirs, the establishment of the American Guild of Organists, an increase in choir schools, increased consolidation of hymnody, and a rise in professional church music training all laid a foundation for his own thinking. His ideas also resonated with certain contemporary thinkers like Erik Routley, who in a 1966 discussion of American trends talked about the "vast and amiable vulgarity about much that goes on in the practice of church music," along with a "virtuoso-cult" that threatens to turn churches into concert halls, and which needs to be tempered by liturgy and theology.[55]

At the same time, several other contemporary figures took very different approaches. The 20th Century Church Light Music Group, established in the late 1950s by several British musicians, promoted hymns and other pieces in folk and other lighter styles, using dance rhythms and pop-oriented harmonies. The Second Vatican Council, though officially privileging Gregorian chant, propagated a range of contemporary Catholic music in vernacular languages and accessible styles. Several other movements toward folk, jazz, and popular music with heavy congregational participation also flew in the face of Sowerby's vision. And as mentioned earlier, some of this thinking would make its way directly into the 1982 Episcopal *Hymnal* as a repudiation of Sowerby's views.

Even so, Sowerby's writings offer a glimpse into a musician who drew upon the full spectrum of his sacred environment to craft an integrated—if somewhat elitist—philosophy of church music. If certain aspects of his authoritarian aesthetics might nowadays seem old-fashioned, given the widespread presence of multiculturalism, inclusivity, and popular styles in many churches, his views nonetheless stand as a monument to the importance of high artistry in sacred music.

An additional consequence of Sowerby's growing church music preoccupations of the 1940s and 1950s is that his thoughts on musical modernism took on a more theological slant. As a younger composer focused on the concert hall, Sowerby's notions of modern music centered on "the folk element" as a timeless, native tradition from which composers could draw new inspiration (as observed in chapter 2). But in his later years, as concerns with the present and future of church music became increasingly paramount, Sowerby refashioned his modernist notions to connect them more closely to the Christian worship tradition.

Though acknowledging the troubling reaction that the phrase "modern music" can produce both within and outside the church, Sowerby insisted upon its necessity. As he describes in *Ideals in Church Music*, "Just as it is right and natural that the composer of today should express himself in the idiom of today, so it is right and natural that his work, if it measure up to the proper standards, should be performed today—not tomorrow—for only by trial and error will that which is most worthy be discovered."[56] He invokes another American church composer, David McK. Williams, in asserting that a composer who "plays safe" and thinks only of past compositional models will never be a creative artist, and furthermore that it is the church's duty to encourage artists to speak in modernist idioms.[57] But even as they do, tradition must always maintain a foothold in the modern composer's consciousness; for Sowerby the living composer, "if he be sincere and wise . . . will be guided by tradition, without being a slave to it, and he will not despise the lessons of the past."[58]

The idea of growth is also essential to Sowerby's modernist position, and here again he views the issue through a sacred lens. Music cannot simply retread past styles, as happened for instance with the Catholic *Motu Proprio* of 1903. That edict maintained the primacy of Gregorian chant and Renaissance polyphony over later polyphonic styles, allowing for certain modern compositions but scorning theatrical or otherwise profane influences. Sowerby appreciates the beauty of Gregorian chant, as a hallowed ancient musical practice; but he faults this approach because it offers "no hope for growth, and that music cannot and shall not be reflective of the changes that time itself imposes."[59] This emphasis on contemporary relevance is further reflected in his dismissive perspective on modern Catholic music, which under the *Motu Proprio*'s influence has resulted in "the manufacture of mass after mass, based on Gregorian themes, lacking an inspirational basis, and out of harmony with their own epoch, masses not worthy to be placed beside the music on which they were modelled—the ancient plainsong."[60]

By the same token, there are dangers in becoming *too* individualist in one's music. When Sowerby proclaims, in his essay on composition in relation to the American church, that his current time is "the age of the Individualist," he is not altogether endorsing this view. His concern is that the modern cult of the individual leads people to believe all perspectives are equally valid, despite their comparative lack of cultural or ecclesiastical knowledge, and moreover that much of this music is too heavily focused on individual gratification, rather than to the glory of God.[61]

In "The Compleat Choirmaster," Sowerby reiterates some of these ideas as part of a larger discussion on church authority and the proper disposition of music within the church.[62] But in addressing the particular question of modernism he also cites several paragraphs from a 1935 address by Williams entitled "The Modernist in Church Music."[63] Williams highlights certain tensions between secular and sacred modernism, while also illustrating the need for both contemporary originality and for connecting to the past. Sowerby quotes him:

> What is the future of Church music? It is without doubt in the hands of the so-called *Modernist*. And what is a Modernist? Is he, according to the popular idea, an iconoclast? No indeed; he is quite the opposite. He is a builder, who builds with the material of *today* so that his work may be used *tomorrow*. He is the *only creative* artist. Those who think in terms of yesterday will forever hold the wrong opinion of the modernist. The Modernist of today becomes the classicist of tomorrow. He is the seer, the prophet, the sincere believer in himself, who can express himself only in terms of his own experience. . . . The Modernist, too, has an unfailing reverence for the work on the past, and, in a way, makes himself personally responsible for carrying the ancient standards to still greater heights. . . . I believe that venturesomeness is the most vital quality in art, as well as in living; and it is this element of venturesomeness that is always in evidence in the work of the Modernist.[64]

Here, and indeed throughout Sowerby's own writings, a dialogue between present and past is again in evidence. If a composer's technical arsenal must be contemporary in a "venturesome" sense, he nevertheless cannot be an iconoclast; he must rather be always mindful of his historical lineage. And if Sowerby's sense of history was earlier rooted in American folk elements as a secular composer, his later emphasis on sacred music seems to have recalibrated his focus, in that the tradition of Christian musical worship now proves decisive in shaping his modernist views.

Sowerby and David McK. Williams (Courtesy of the Special Collections Research Center, Syracuse University Libraries).

Sowerby's waning reputation in the concert hall after World War II was not necessarily a conscious decision on his part to withdraw. Rapidly changing conditions within the music world itself, combined with Sowerby's determination to be himself without catering to the latest fashions, left him ill-suited for further success. Alan Rich, writing in 1963 about a Philadelphia Orchestra performance in New York of Sowerby's Organ Concerto in C, captured the crux of the issue: "It's been a long time since Leo Sowerby has gotten the handsome attention he received at Philharmonic Hall last night. It is probably a measure of how quickly things have changed in American music since 1937, rather than any fault of Sowerby himself, that his Organ Concerto sounded a little dated on this occasion. In most ways, however, it is still a very handsome piece."[65]

In sacred music, however, Sowerby came to be regarded over this same period as a transformational figure. As an organ composer he was called " a mystic" who "works his magic with new applications of the technical devices of counterpoint," and elsewhere he was labeled "surely the outstanding composer of music for the

Anglican church in this country, if not indeed the finest of all church music of any denomination."[66] He also developed a new perspective on modernism, rooted in relationships between past and present and guided specifically by theological concerns. Such a blending of sacred and secular invites deeper thinking about modernism in general, and how perspectives of religious composers might fit uneasily within its traditional aesthetics. Cornerstone modernist ideas such as a radical break between modern and premodern, or the glorification of an individual artist's subjective experience, contrast sharply with the religiously informed approach of a figure like Sowerby. And if secular modernists might be inclined to reject such approaches as not being aesthetically self-sufficient, the fact that Sowerby and other sacred composers firmly identified themselves as modernists should at least prompt further consideration of their voices.

# Washington and the College of Church Musicians (1962–68)

**AT FIRST GLANCE IT MIGHT APPEAR SHOCKING** for a lifelong Chicagoan, firmly ensconced among the city's musical leaders, to suddenly pick up stakes and move to a new city. To do so at an age when many others are gratefully anticipating retirement is all the more striking. But for Sowerby, whose commitment to quality sacred music had strengthened appreciably over several decades, the opportunity to lead a school that could permanently enshrine his perspectives proved irresistible. Already a veteran teacher from his American Conservatory years, and well established in church music circles as both an outstanding practical musician and a supreme intellectual authority, Sowerby was a natural choice to lead a new institution devoted to intensive, graduate-level education in church music.

The College of Church Musicians (CCM) was an experimental project based out of Washington National Cathedral that hoped to build a new type of center for advanced church music study. Its mission was threefold: (1) to offer specialized, advanced training to unusually qualified students in worship music; (2) to become a national center for organists, choirmasters, and clergy to attend seminars and discuss problems related to worship music; and (3) to stimulate creative and experimental works of church music. These values aligned very closely with Sowerby's own church music priorities, and although its efforts were ultimately short-lived, the CCM exerted a lasting influence through both the ideals it espoused and the students who graduated from its program.

## History and Development of the CCM

The idea of a collegiate church music institute had been floating around for nearly a decade prior to the CCM's actual founding. Its origins can be traced to Easter Week of 1953, when the cathedral hosted a Colloquium on the Training of Church Musicians at which several musicians discussed strategies for building sacred music programs through church-led initiatives. Sowerby himself spoke at this meeting, leading a discussion on "The Education of the Church Musician" during which he complained that traditional music schools neglected to teach the essential practical skills required of church musicians—things like service playing, improvisation, repertory selection, choir organization and management, and sacred music composition.[1]

Out of this symposium emerged a scheme for establishing a collegiate institution, ecumenical in nature and based at the cathedral itself. Washington was well positioned musically to support such an initiative, with two internationally renowned musical leaders in music director Paul Callaway and assistant organist Richard Wayne Dirksen, along with several high-quality choruses including a men and boys choir, the Cathedral Choral Society, and the glee clubs of Saint Albans School and the National Cathedral School for Girls. On April 18, 1953, the cathedral chapter authorized Dean Francis Bowes Sayre Jr. to devise preliminary plans for such a college, and Sayre worked with Callaway over the next several years to secure financial support. Seven years later, on October 24, 1960, the trustees of the National Cathedral Association formally approved the CCM's creation and offered to supply the necessary support for its founding. Dirksen and Admiral Neill Phillips, president of the National Cathedral Association, drew up plans for a three-year pilot program, and in spring 1962 Sayre announced the formal opening of the college, with Sowerby as its director.[2]

It would be reasonable to ask why Sowerby would choose to make such a dramatic life change at this point. Besides the comfort associated with long-term settlement in a dynamic city, Sowerby's salary at Saint James had risen to around $10,000—a quite respectable sum, considering that the median US family income for 1962 was around $6,000.[3] Yet aside from what must have been a compelling desire to lead an institution that could secure his legacy, Sowerby was deeply invested in issues of church music pedagogy. In particular, he sought the return of an apprentice model that focused on the needs of actual working musicians. In an interview for the cathedral's official magazine *Cathedral Age*, Sowerby claimed this model was something American institutions had themselves espoused until about a generation ago, after which the growth of professional "schools of music" led to a new emphasis on academic degrees for teaching. And in yet another instance of his connection to tradition, he invoked a long history of success with similar systems that had produced such renowned church musicians as Palestrina, Byrd, Buxtehude, Bach, and Schubert.[4]

There were other, more personal factors involved in the decision to move. Sowerby's doctor had advised him against maintaining his dual careers at the American Conservatory and at Saint James, due to issues with hypertension, and in fact he had passed along most of his day-to-day Saint James organ duties to his assistant. Personal correspondence with his student William Ferris, who studied with Sowerby from 1957 to 1962, also reveals a certain dissatisfaction that had crept into his final years—a sense he was not being supported musically, and that emerging trends toward more popular sacred music styles were incompatible with his ethos.[5] In a letter dated July 24, 1962, written while at Camp Wa-Li-Ro, Sowerby tells Ferris that he has been working hard and making up for lost time, because "as you know, it was impossible during my last few months in Chicago to do anything." Later letters reveal a sense of regret and dismay, especially regarding his successors at Saint James. In one, dated January 28, 1965, Sowerby laments what was evidently an inferior performance of his choral piece "Tu es vas electionis": "I just cannot understand what's gotten into them there; apparently, it's just as though I had never been there. . . . It's apparent that I'm being quickly forgotten in Chicago, except by a few of my close personal friends. But I didn't expect to be forgotten so soon at St. James'!"

The inauguration service for the CCM took place on September 16, 1962. In his sermon preached on the occasion, Sayre emphasized the advantages of students being educated in a worship environment rather than a university, as well as the elevated quality of artistry that would be expected of them. CCM students were already advanced technical musicians; what the college offered was a liturgical environment in which their music could bring people closer to God through worship and praise. "This is not something, obviously, to be learned in a classroom any more than the Holy Spirit is met in a book of theology," Sayre stated. "Rather, it is a precision of spirit that is caught: caught through exposure to a milieu in which music is not allowed just to float about seeking some new sensation, or to pander to the habitual predilections of the crowd, but where men of music strive for that integrity that is close to the truth of God."[6]

Fellows of the CCM were limited to around fifteen in number—only seven for the first year—and were chosen on a competitive basis. A previous music degree was not mandatory, but applicants were expected to be unusually gifted musicians, with organ skills sufficient to take the American Guild of Organists' associateship certification exam. They were also expected to demonstrate serious commitment to their vocation as church musicians, and applications were open to all regardless of race, national origin, or religious faith. All fellows received scholarships for the duration of their studies, which could last anywhere from one to three years.

Once at the CCM, fellows received a broad-based education in liturgy, hymnody, plainsong and Anglican chant, service music, advanced organ studies, composition, analysis and orchestration, along with practical guidance for recruiting, training, and administering choirs. The faculty was a small but elite corps: Sowerby himself taught composition and demanded that students compose original works, which were often then performed in the Cathedral's services. Dirksen and Callaway served as organ and conducting faculty, while musicologist Leonard Ellinwood taught music history and Reverend William C. Workman, the Cathedral's

The first class of students from the College of Church Musicians: Sowerby, Beverly Ward (standing), Charles Bradley, John Cooper, Ronald Rice, William ("Pat") Partridge, Roger Petrich (Courtesy of the Leo Sowerby Foundation).

canon precentor, taught liturgy. The advisory board included several big names: composers Samuel Barber and Howard Hanson, conductor Eugene Ormandy, organist/composer Alec Wyton.

Performance was of course essential to the fellows' training. They gave their own recitals on the cathedral's great organ, and they also regularly played continuo lines from figured bass for orchestral performances of Baroque repertory. They worked in rehearsal and performance with the cathedral's various choirs, and further benefited from workshops and seminars with visiting musicians of prominence.

With all its benefits, however, the CCM also had its struggles. Finances were an issue from the start, and the college's existence was in many ways a year-to-year proposition. Internal politics also dogged the institution at times. The organist, Dirksen in particular, was critical of the college's workings, assailing at various points its recruitment practices, its administrative shortcomings, the undue burdens placed on faculty, problematic faculty-student relationships, and the lack of public recognition of collegiate activities. Although these philosophical difficulties were ultimately worked out, the CCM's finances remained insecure (a problem also shared by the cathedral at large), and the institution closed down in 1969, not long after Sowerby's own passing.

Upon moving to Washington Sowerby lodged in a house on the cathedral grounds at 2920 34th Street NW. Though small, it was nonetheless larger than his Chicago apartment and allowed him for the first time to keep his books and music in one place. When this house was razed in 1965, he shared expenses on a new place (3210 Wisconsin Avenue NW, #702) with one of his CCM students, Ronald Stalford. He settled into a routine in which composition typically happened in the morning along with personal correspondence and other business, while teaching occurred in the afternoon. At the conclusion of daily Evensong, which let out at 4:30 p.m., Sowerby returned home for dinner, social drinking, and reading. Initially Stalford lived somewhat separately from Sowerby, but he became increasingly integrated into this routine—often cooking dinner, and eventually becoming Sowerby's primary caretaker as illnesses took hold.

William "Pat" Partridge, who has been canon precentor, organist, and choirmaster at Christ Church Cathedral in St. Louis for more than forty years, was part of the first class of fellows to enter the CCM. In an interview for this book he spoke with great fondness about his time with Sowerby, discussing various aspects of his compositional studies and his personal impressions.

There were seven of us there for that first two years, we all had at least once a week a private session with Dr. Leo. We all tried our hand at it, but our sessions would be about the analysis of music. Learning how to think before you write something. He was just a master at analyzing, any kind of music.

No one actually studied organ with him—that was the duty of Paul Callaway; it was his job to be the organ professor. But we all played Dr. Leo's music, we all had to play a recital during the first and second years, we could talk to him about his own pieces. We actually wished that would happen occasionally. He talked in those sessions about his life at Saint James', and how he went through preparing for and scheduling music, and that was of great interest to me and everyone else because he had done it for so long.[7]

The fellows highly valued Sowerby's teaching ability, from his encyclopedic knowledge of repertory to his uncompromising performance standards. Never one to categorize his own style, Sowerby also avoided indoctrinating his students into any particular mold and held up excellence as his only priority. As Partridge relates,

Oh my goodness, he was a wonderful teacher of anything. Dr. Leo in those late years, he was . . . his life had quieted down. I was told by people who knew him back then [in Chicago] that he was a taskmaster, could lose his temper and did easily, was just so demanding. He was demanding of us, but in a quiet way. He could just bring things out of you, get in a conversation and ask you questions. . . . He tried hard to analyze the music personality of all seven of us, and then turn it around. His patience was quite wonderful back then.

Partridge's impressions of Sowerby's personal qualities were similarly effusive, giving a sense of close familiarity and a sincere devotion to those in his community.

Kindly—first word. To us, to everyone I saw him with. I used to travel with him to do workshops and master classes, he took me along as accompanist. I was always so amazed how kindly and patient he was with everyone he was dealing with. Sometimes you get not-too-good choirs, but he was always so kindly and patient.

I used to take him shopping up the street from the cathedral, I'd drive him up there to get his groceries; he liked to go off by himself. He loved round steak and Brussels sprouts, and I remember we came home and he said to help him unpack. He went and turned on the oven to high, took out the big slabs of steak, then just went off and left them. He also really loved his happy hours, and his martinis.

## Other Activities and Final Years

Sowerby's Washington years were hardly a respite. He was busy as ever with teaching, composing, conducting, lecturing, and various travel obligations, including trips back to his Palisades Park lakeside cottage whenever possible—often after his summer engagements at Wa-Li-Ro. Honors continued to be bestowed as well. One major accolade occurred in 1963, when Sowerby was named a fellow of the Royal School of Church Music in England—the first American to be granted such a designation. He was also elected to the Council of the American Guild of Organists in 1965, having put himself up for candidacy upon the strong recommendation of his friend Alec Wyton.

Perhaps naturally, his compositional activity during these final years emphasized choral and organ works. Dozens of choral anthems for wide-ranging vocal forces, along with sundry organ preludes, postludes, and other works, characterize his Washingtonian output. Many of these were composed for specific dedications or commemorations, and their complexity reflects Sowerby's continued interest in high-quality repertory. A prominent example of this type is "Christians to the Paschal Victim," a large-scale anthem composed in September 1965 for Callaway and the cathedral choir as they embarked on a two-week trip to London for the Festival of American Arts and Humanities.

Other works, in contrast, are simpler in scope and offer good opportunities for less advanced choirs to "sing Sowerby." These include a series of anthems and service music for reduced vocal scoring, intended specifically for the boys choir at Wa-Li-Ro, as well as an array of hymn tunes. In deference to emerging worship trends, Sowerby also wrote certain pieces with broader ideals in mind, such as music for the Catholic mass with newly approved English-language texts. Sowerby's cultivation of Catholic music was particularly motivated by his close friendship with *Washington Post* critic Paul Hume, a Catholic as well as an instructor at Georgetown University. Across 1965 and 1966 he wrote two mass settings (one a unison setting, the other SATB), as well as myriad settings of the Gradual and Alleluia.

Among the most notable of Sowerby's final choral works is "Thy Word Is a Lantern unto My Feet," a memorial response to the November 22, 1963, assassination of President John Fitzgerald Kennedy. As a lifelong Democrat who greatly esteemed the Kennedy and Roosevelt families ("his admiration for John Kennedy was endless," according to Preston Rockholt, organist and director of studies at the CCM), Sowerby was deeply distressed by Kennedy's assassination, and he noted in a letter to his student Ferris that his anthem "certainly was deeply felt!"[8] The anthem was premiered at a special concert with the William Ferris Chorale in Washington on June 12, 1965, celebrating his own seventy-fifth birthday.[9] Its text, drawn from Psalm 119, resounds with parallels between the spiritual guidance offered by God and Kennedy's own perceived leadership qualities: "Thy word is a lantern unto my feet, and a light unto my paths. / Thou art my defense and shield; and my trust is thy word." Stylistically, the anthem represents vintage Sowerby in many respects. Chromatic harmonies, frequently dense sonorities, and a blending of imitative/fugal polyphony and homorhythm characterize the piece. Homophonic declaration in particular is used for dramatic textual emphasis, on phrases like "and my trust is in thy word" and "show the light of thy countenance upon thy servant."

Secular music also emerged even in this final period, including an oboe suite, a piece for wind band and carillon, and art song settings of Emily Dickinson texts. Two large-scale concert works—the Symphony No. 5 (1964) and a second concerto for organ and orchestra (1968)—demonstrate Sowerby's continued interest in large-scale secular forms. Neither of these received public performances, however, though as late as December 1964 Sowerby was in correspondence with Eugene Ormandy about having the Philadelphia Orchestra premiere the symphony.[10]

On November 15, 1965, Sowerby was granted a $2,500 commission from the Serge Koussevitzky Music Foundation to compose a large-scale work for chorus and orchestra.[11] The product of this commission was his last major work: *La Corona*, a twenty-two-minute, single-movement cantata for tenor soloist, chorus, and orchestra. He completed the sketch on December 19, 1966, yet orchestration proved difficult because of lingering health troubles. As late as two days before his death he mentioned in a letter his desire to keep working on the piece, but completing the orchestration ultimately fell to his former student Ferris. The premiere occurred only on April 28, 1990, part of a year-long celebration of the final stone setting at Washington Cathedral.

*La Corona* sets the "La Corona" sonnets of John Donne, a cycle of seven poems (La Corona—Annunciation—Nativity—Temple—Crucifixion—Resurrection—Ascension) that meditate on the story of Christ's life and redemption. Several aspects of circularity are emphasized. Donne's poetry traces Christ's journey from his conception in heaven, to his life on earth, and then back to his heavenly ascension. The poems further invoke the symbol of an unbroken crown through their circular form, in which the final line of each poem is repeated as the first line of the next (with the very last line of the final poem a repeat of the first line of the initial poem). Sowerby's musical setting reflects this scheme by using the same melody for each paired textual repetition, though with differing pitch levels, harmonies, and textures. He further reflects Donne's fourteen-line poetic scheme by inserting orchestral interludes between the octave and sestet for each poem.

At several points, Sowerby accentuates the words' prosody and dramatizes their emotional content. Example 8, taken from the fourth poem "Temple" (which depicts the twelve-year-old Christ in discussion with the learned doctors), illus-

Example 8. *La Corona*, H.466, mm. 188–97

trates this expressiveness. As Jesus's remarkable learning is revealed, the music shifts from a unison declaration on "blowing sparks of wit" with the elders to increasingly complex homophony, leading to an aching melodic and dynamic climax on the "Word" being spoken. The bafflement of a boy suddenly able to "speak wonders" is depicted with a combination of softer dynamics ("holding back") and a large-scale rising melodic ascent.

Beyond these music-text relations, other favored Sowerby devices such as tonal ambiguity, chromatic enrichment, fugue, and alternation between contrapuntal and homophonic choral textures are all present, though perhaps with less intensity than in some earlier works. Indeed, the overriding sentiment conveyed by the piece is a kind of autumnal warmth, a contented resignation that perhaps was on Sowerby's own mind during the composition process.

Despite Sowerby's commitment to pursuing his composing and teaching with as much vigor as before, health issues increasingly impinged on these activities. Around Christmastime of 1964 Sowerby was hospitalized for a prostate operation in New York City, which was followed by a lengthy rest period. In autumn 1966 he suffered yet another illness, and toward Christmas that year became afflicted with shingles. On January 16, 1967, he suffered congestive heart failure, which kept him hospitalized for nearly two weeks. His recovery was then affected by a stroke on February 16, which sent him to the hospital for another week. Though determined to continue composing, his activities were limited by continued physical pain, to the point of barely being able to finger a five-note scale.

Although Sowerby eventually regained some of his strength, he continued to be afflicted by small strokes as well as diabetes. And in the early morning of Sunday, July 7, 1968, while at Wa-Li-Ro for his usual summer work, he suffered a massive stroke. His friend Warren Miller, who had been caring for him at this camp, found him unable to speak intelligibly, and although he was rushed to a nearby hospital at Port Clinton, Ohio, he was pronounced dead at 4:25 p.m. Stalford flew out immediately to Ohio and arranged for Sowerby's cremation. The ashes were mailed back parcel post (albeit with some delays), and Sowerby was interred in the columbarium of Washington Cathedral on July 10.

Memorial services were conducted in Chicago, Washington, New York, and elsewhere. At Saint James in Chicago a special memorial mass was given on July 10, headed by Dean William Maxwell. Plans were delayed in Washington, however, because so many of Sowerby's associates were away for the summer. The memorial ultimately took place on October 19, with service music consisting almost entirely of Sowerby's own compositions (keyboard works *Passacaglia for Carillon*, the first movement of the Organ Symphony, and *Requiescat in Pace*, plus choral anthems "Psalm 122," "I Will Love Thee, O Lord," and "Tu es vas electionis") performed by Sowerby students and colleagues.

In New York, a service at Saint Thomas Church was held on October 27. Washington Cathedral Dean Sayre came up from Washington to deliver the sermon, and in comparing Sowerby's gifts to those of the biblical figure of David he perhaps captured most eloquently the nature of Sowerby's achievements.

What was the quality of David's life that made him so long remembered? And the like quality in Sowerby? Was it not that they both were born to such simplicity—which they never lost until they died?

But yet each could rise to such complexity!—could encompass such a wealth of stunning offertory: which they also rendered to the Lord, having mixed the maturity of their minds and hearts and wills and memories with the haunting melody of youth.

Was it not this paradox of simultaneity, this combining of the plain with the utterly ingenious—that characterized their praise? . . .

Nevertheless, we remember not his music only, but his gracious life among us as well. His whole being was a psalm: of humble love and friendship, of keen and discerning intelligence! of passionate dedication to our Heavenly Father, whom he worshipped with all his heart, . . . soul, . . . and mind.[12]

# Epilogue

## *Forgetting and Remembering*

In the immediate wake of Sowerby's death, encomiums poured in extolling his virtues. Many of these tributes emphasized Sowerby's achievements in sacred music, while acknowledging his overall versatility of achievement. Lawrence Sears wrote in the *Washington Evening Star* that, while Sowerby "was prolific in virtually every field except opera . . . [o]rgan and choral music were his special realm."[1] The October 1968 symposium of tribute in *Music: The A.G.O.-R.C.C.O. Magazine*, referenced in this book's introduction, illustrates the wide reach of his influence—concert organist E. Power Biggs, church organist/choirmaster Ned Gammons, composer Howard Hanson, critic Paul Hume, publisher Donald Gray, and student Gerre Hancock all penned contributions.

Sowerby's reputation in sacred music has stood the test of time, and his music—especially his organ repertory—continues to be admired and performed regularly. Its technical difficulties often prove a barrier to entry for less accomplished musicians, but investing in this music can produce great rewards. In an interview for this book, Stephen Buzard discussed some of the obstacles faced by musicians approaching Sowerby. "Learning Sowerby is a bit like learning [Max] Reger," Buzard observes. "At first, the music seems dense and uninviting until you uncover the structure, nuance, and expressive power of the piece. Without patience and trust, it can feel daunting to learn a new work of Sowerby. For that reason, I feel like I never gave his music a fair shake until I came to Chicago. I hope others will not make my mistake!"[2]

Buzard regularly programs Sowerby's music for the weekly liturgies at Saint James, as well as his own organ concert tours. In doing so, he recognizes a number of features that make both the organ and choral repertory distinctive. "Sowerby uses the organ in a fully symphonic way, calling for a wide variety of tonal colors and great expressive capability. Registrations are ever-shifting like a kaleidoscope, requiring a high degree of console technique from the player," he notes. At the same time, the organ part is essential to a full understanding of Sowerby's choral music. "[Sowerby] conducted the Saint James choir from the console, and the function of the organ in his music is to lead the singers rather than merely to support. Like the lieder of Schumann, the organ often has the 'last word,' adding meaning beyond the text."

Vocally as well, Sowerby's choral music presents certain distinctive features relative to the Anglican repertory to which it is so often compared. As Buzard notes, "Unlike most English composers, Sowerby wrote for adult professional singers. As a result, he calls for longer lines and more technical challenges than in the music of his contemporaries across the pond. Sowerby also wrote for dry American spaces, and the length of his vocal phrases help simulate the sense of space and grandeur that comes naturally in a rolling acoustic."

Some of Sowerby's music might even be construed as scandalous, depending on one's point of view. As Buzard describes:

> Sowerby's harmonic style feels like it skirts the boundaries of what could be considered seemly or appropriate in church. I joke with the choir that Psalm 122 sounds like [Hubert] Parry went to a speakeasy! Yet it is so delightful—and sanctifying—that Sowerby brought the sounds of the street into the church. When I hear his music, I imagine Chicago in the thirties and forties with all of its swagger, its chaos, and its problems. That world is not so very far from our own and helps explain how we got to now.

If Sowerby remains a respected figure in church music, his concert music is seldom performed; the trend toward reduced visibility described in chapter 4 has certainly carried into the twenty-first century. Yet recent decades have also seen various efforts to bring Sowerby to greater public notice, often led by former students or associates and centered on the city of Chicago. In February 1986, former Sowerby student William Ferris spearheaded a series of events that included an all-Sowerby organ recital; a roundtable discussion "Remembering Leo" with various friends and colleagues from the Chicago Symphony, the American Conservatory, and Saint James Cathedral; and a concert with the William Ferris Chorale featuring "Thy Word Is a Lantern unto My Feet," *The Throne of God*, and the Classic Concerto for Organ and Strings.[3] A Newberry Library exhibit of Sowerby manuscripts and memorabilia accompanied the occasion. In 1989, pianist and former Sowerby student Gail Quillman organized a Chicago concert series of Sowerby's piano works and recorded a CD of several of these pieces. The next year, on the anniversary of Sowerby's ninety-fifth birthday, Chicago mayor Richard Daley proclaimed the month of May Leo Sowerby Month, part of an eight-week festival of concerts, recordings, and exhibitions involving both sacred and secular repertoire. The year 1995 marked the centennial of the composer's birth, about which *New York Times* reporter Sarah Bryan Miller remarked that Sowerby was enjoying a "modest comeback," thanks to concerts sponsored by the Leo Sowerby Foundation and a spate of CD releases. The Leo Sowerby Foundation, based in Kilgore, Texas, has issued dozens of previously unpublished Sowerby scores, supported public performances and recordings, and promoted Sowerby's music through its own YouTube channel.

One of the major forces in bringing Sowerby to renewed visibility is Cedille Records, a not-for-profit record label devoted to Chicago-area classical musicians. Since 1997 Cedille has issued nine recordings containing Sowerby repertory, focusing especially on concert repertories that have not previously been recorded and featuring a range of solo, chamber, and orchestral ensembles. In 2020, Cedille included in the "Discover" section of its website a special tribute to Sowerby on the occasion of his 125th birthday, reflecting on the composer's legacy and the label's own history of recording Sowerby's works.[4] The label also marketed summer 2021 as the "Summer of Sowerby," with three albums in a row featuring Sowerby's music performed by various Chicago musicians (the Lincoln Trio, the Andy Baker Orchestra, the Avalon String Quartet, keyboardist David Schrader).

In an interview for this book Jim Ginsburg, Cedille's president, discussed several of the factors behind his interest in recording Sowerby.

> Sowerby is one of the great exemplars of the American Romantic tradition alongside his friends and admirers Samuel Barber and Howard Hanson. He has a distinctive voice with his characteristic, even unique, harmonies and chord progressions, yet the variety of styles among his compositions is vast. He's one of those composers who, like one of his musical idols, Stravinsky, it seems sought never to write the "same" work twice (while still maintaining his own identifiable voice, even if he himself could not identify it). His music is both intellectually and emotionally moving and satisfying. I believe this comes from the masterful use of form and counterpoint that undergirds his compositions.[5]

Ginsburg notes that many of Cedille's recordings have happened alongside live performance projects, which have helped boost Sowerby's concert profile, and that several Cedille artists who previously knew little about Sowerby are now seeking out other works for future performance. Additional recordings of Sowerby are also in store ("There definitely will be more Sowerby," Ginsburg says), including a recording by Chicago Pro Musica of the wind quintet that will likely become part of an all-Chicago (or at least all-American) wind quintets album.

Asked why he believes Sowerby is an important figure to preserve on recordings, Ginsburg gives a straightforward answer: "Music this good needs to be preserved. I also hope that our recordings will lead to more performances of his music as well as a reevaluation that puts him in his proper place at least alongside other twentieth-century American 'Romantic' composers."

Although Ginsburg's comments focus primarily on Sowerby's status as a secular composer, continued reevaluation of his legacy might also take up an even larger issue: how religiously minded composers fit into broader historiographies of modern music history. Modern sacred music is sometimes seen as occupying a separate narrative from that of concert hall repertories, lacking the requisite aesthetic independence for consideration as works of "art." Religious works—especially music meant for practical, liturgical performance—are seemingly too constrained by the conditions of sacred worship to stand alongside secular music, which in the current day can pursue limitless creative, intellectual, and technological directions.

Another complication emerges from the proscriptive qualities associated with "sacred" and "secular" labels. Although certainly there are plenty of composers who write strictly for sacred worship, and many others who avoid this field entirely, Sowerby himself defies easy categorization. Does the fact that Sowerby composed so much sacred music, and was himself religious, identify him by default as a "sacred" composer? And does this identification condition us to diminish his "art" composer status, despite the large volume of secular works produced by his pen?

Ultimately, of course, the question of forgetting or remembering extends beyond any single figure. Efforts to recover "lost" voices have taken high priority in recent times, in particular the long-overdue attention now being paid to musicians from more diverse gender, racial, and stylistic backgrounds. Twentieth-century composers like Sowerby, Hanson, Harris, and Barber, who cultivated traditional musical forms and who don't necessarily fall within the abovementioned demographic profiles, may not appear fashionable amid this milieu. Yet their music remains capable of speaking to today's listeners, and indeed greater familiarity with it is essential to appreciating the construction of America's national music tradition.

# NOTES

*Introduction*

1. "Leo Sowerby: A Symposium of Tribute," *Music: The A.G.O.-R.C.C.O. Magazine* 51 (October 1968): 27.

2. "Leo Sowerby: A Symposium of Tribute," 65.

3. Stephen Buzard, "On Big Shoulders: Learning Sowerby at St. James Cathedral, Chicago," *Vox Humana*, October 20, 2017, accessed March 12, 2020, http://www.voxhumana-journal.com/buzard2017.html.

4. Henry Cowell, *American Composers on American Music* (1933; 2nd ed. New York: Frederick Ungar, 1962), 9.

5. Carol Oja, "A Forgotten Vanguard: The Legacy of Marion Bauer, Frederick Jacobi, Emerson Whithorne, and Louis Gruenberg," in *Making Music Modern: New York in the 1920s* (New York: Oxford University Press, 2000), 155–76; and Oja, "Forging an International Alliance: Leo Sowerby, Elizabeth Sprague Coolidge, and the Impact of a Rome Prize," in *Music and Musical Composition at the American Academy in Rome*, ed. Martin Brody (Rochester, NY: University of Rochester Press, 2014), 196.

6. As the organist Harold Stover has observed, "like the writers of the period in search of The Great American Novel, many composers dreamed of writing The Great American Symphony." Harold Stover, "Leo Sowerby at 100," *New England Organist* 5, no. 3 (May–June 1995), accessed March 22, 2019, https://www.albany.edu/piporg-l/Sowerby.html. Stover additionally observes that this generation "took the old European forms and poured into them music which sounded distinctly American in its melody, harmony, and rhythm."

7. Andrea Olmstead, "The Rome Prize from Leo Sowerby to David Diamond," in *Music and Musical Composition at the American Academy in Rome*, ed. Martin Brody (Rochester, NY: University of Rochester Press, 2014), 16.

8. On *Prairie* see Beth Levy, *Frontier Figures: American Music and the Mythology of the American West* (Berkeley: University of California Press, 2012), 161–67. On *The Canticle of the Sun* see Joseph Sargent, "Forgetting and Remembering: The Case of Leo Sowerby's 'The Canticle of the Sun,'" *American Music* 38, no. 4 (Winter 2020): 485–517. Among theses and dissertations focusing on Sowerby's music, the central reference is Ronald M. Huntington, "A Study of the Musical Contributions of Leo Sowerby" (MM thesis, University of Southern California, 1957). Other Sowerby-centered studies include O. G. Parks, "A

Critical Analysis of the Works of Leo Sowerby" (MM thesis, North Texas State Teachers College, 1941); B. Wayne Hinds, "Leo Sowerby: A Biography and Descriptive Listing of Anthems" (EdD thesis, Georgia Peabody College for Teachers, 1972); Raymond Durward Jones, "Leo Sowerby: His Life and His Choral Music" (PhD diss., University of Iowa, 1973); and Brice Gerlach, "Leo Sowerby's *The Canticle of the Sun*: An Analysis for Performance (DM diss., Indiana University, 2008).

9. See, for instance, Francis Crociata, liner notes to *Prairie: Tone Poems by Leo Sowerby*, Czech National Symphony Orchestra, Paul Freeman, conductor, Cedille Records CDR 90000 033, 1997, compact disc; and Crociata, liner notes to *Leo Sowerby: Symphony No. 2, Passacaglia, Interlude & Fugue, Concert Overture, All on a Summer's Day*, Chicago Sinfonietta and Czech National Symphony Orchestra, Paul Freeman, conductor, Cedille Records CDR 90000 039, 1998, compact disc.

10. See for instance F.D., "Leo Sowerby's Program," *Chicago Daily Tribune*, January 19, 1917, II5; Gilbert Chase, *America's Music*, 2nd rev. ed. (New York: McGraw-Hill, 1966), 551; Randall Thompson, "The Contemporary Scene in American Music," *Musical America* 52 (April 25, 1932): 12; and Timothy W. Sharp, "The Choral Music of Leo Sowerby: A Centennial Perspective," *Choral Journal* 35, no. 8 (1995): 14.

11. Quoted in John Tasker Howard, *Our Contemporary Composers: American Music in the Twentieth Century* (New York: Thomas Y. Crowell, 1941), 80.

12. Howard, *Our Contemporary Composers*, 81. For other references to this phrase see Robert Rayfield, liner notes to *Sowerby at Trinity*, Faythe Freese, organ, Albany Records Troy 368, 2000, compact disc; and Parks, "A Critical Analysis of the Works of Leo Sowerby," 16.

13. Howard, *Our Contemporary Composers*, 81.

14. Lawrence P. Schreiber, "Leo Sowerby," *Music Journal Anthology* (Annual, 1967), 1–2.

15. Rayfield, liner notes to *Sowerby at Trinity*.

16. E. Power Biggs, unpublished notes. Cited in Barbara Owen, *E. Power Biggs, Concert Organist* (Bloomington: Indiana University Press, 1987), 50.

17. Burnet C. Tuthill, "Leo Sowerby," *Musical Quarterly* 24 (1938): 251.

18. Huntington, "A Study of the Musical Contributions of Sowerby"; Marilois Kierman, "The Compositions of Leo Sowerby for Organ Solo" (MM thesis, American University, 1966); Hinds, "Leo Sowerby: A Biography and Descriptive Listing of Anthems"; and Jones, "Leo Sowerby: His Life and His Choral Music." Among other biographical studies, Huntington had started work on a voluminous Sowerby biography, which is now held at the Newberry, but had only reached the year 1917 before passing away. Another biographical sketch, by Chicago writer Rosa Malfitano, is currently housed in a number of collections, including the Sowerby Foundation in Kilgore, Texas, and the Newberry Library. As Huntington detailed in a letter to Jones, Sowerby's own annotations of Huntington's drafts were unfortunately lost to a house fire. See Jones, "Leo Sowerby: His Life and His Choral Music," 3n6.

19. Denise Von Glahn, *The Sounds of Place: Music and the American Cultural Landscape* (Boston: Northeastern University Press, 2003), 2, 7.

20. The critic Glenn Dillard Gunn, writing in the *Chicago Herald and Examiner*, proclaimed in a review of a Sowerby organ recital that "A new school of sacred music is developing in America," led by Sowerby and his colleagues Harvey Gaul and Eric DeLamarter.

See Gunn, "Sowerby's Recital Reveals New Sacred Music School," *Chicago Herald and Examiner*, undated, Leo Sowerby Papers, Special Collections Research Center, Syracuse University Libraries. More recently, John Ogasapian observed about Sowerby's "distinctive and sharply advanced" church music that, "in retrospect, Sowerby's is best seen as a distinctly American idiom in the manner of a Copland, Ives, or even Gershwin. His materials were traditionally European but their use was not." Ogasapian, *Church Music in America, 1620–2000* (Macon, GA: Mercer University Press, 2007), 245.

21. Scholarly conceptions of American music run an extremely wide gamut, from (to take four examples from recent decades) H. Wiley Hitchcock's survey-centered approach of both cultivated and vernacular music "to view our music head-on, to measure it in its own terms, and to seek the 'why' behind the 'what' in American music," to Barbara L. Tischler's emphasis on twentieth-century Americans embracing modernism in full accord with their European peers, to Gann's perspective that "America" in music has less to do with actual musical content and more with common social conditions, to Horowitz's focus on the institutions of classical music and a "culture of performance," under which attention toward an elite group of high-profile interpreters ultimately inhibited American compositional creativity. See Hitchcock, *Music in the United States: A Historical Introduction*, 2nd ed. (Englewood Cliffs, NJ: Prentice-Hall, 1974), ix; Tischler, *An American Music: The Search for an American Musical Identity* (New York and Oxford: Oxford University Press, 1986), 3; Gann, *American Music in the Twentieth Century* (New York: Thomson Wadsworth, 2006), xiv; and Horowitz, *Classical Music in America: A History of Its Rise and Fall* (New York: W. W. Norton, 2005), 265–70.

22. For a recent study of how Sowerby's organ music relates to particular qualities of the organs he used professionally see Mark Evan Stolter, "The Influence of the American Orchestral Organ on Selected Works of Leo Sowerby" (DMA diss., University of Kansas, 2019).

*Chapter 1. The Emerging Americanist (1895–1918)*

1. Huntington, "A Study of the Musical Contributions of Leo Sowerby," 8.

2. Interview with Bertha Wiersma Nolton, Fort Lauderdale, FL, June 22, 1970, in Hinds, "Leo Sowerby: A Biography," 4–5.

3. Interviews with Bertha Nolton and Lillian Sowerby, St. Petersburg, FL, June 24, 1970, in Hinds, "Leo Sowerby: A Biography," 5.

4. Interview with Nolton, in Hinds, "Leo Sowerby: A Biography," 5.

5. Hinds, "Leo Sowerby: A Biography," 5.

6. Sowerby, unpublished/typewritten autobiographical notes, in Hinds, "Leo Sowerby: A Biography," 6.

7. Sowerby, typewritten autobiographical notes, in Jones, "Leo Sowerby: His Life and His Choral Music," 2. Jones observes that Sowerby typed these notes about a year before his death.

8. Interview with Lillian Sowerby, in Hinds, "Leo Sowerby: A Biography," 6.

9. Sowerby interview with Marilois Kierman, in Kierman, "The Compositions of Leo Sowerby for Organ Solo," 1.

10. Jim Ginsburg, host, "Francis Crociata / Leo Sowerby: Selected Works for Solo and Duo Piano," Cedille Classical Chicago Podcast, Episode 33, accessed March 3, 2021, https://www.cedillerecords.org/podcasts/episode-33-francis-crociata-leo-sowerby-selected-works-for-solo-and-duo-piano.

11. Interview with Nolton, in Hinds, "Leo Sowerby: A Biography," 7.

12. Interview with Nolton, in Hinds, "Leo Sowerby: A Biography," 7.

13. Huntington, "A Study of the Musical Contributions of Leo Sowerby," 9.

14. Kierman, "The Compositions of Leo Sowerby for Organ Solo," 2.

15. Sowerby autobiographical notes, in Jones, "Leo Sowerby: His Life and His Choral Music," 4.

16. Sowerby autobiographical notes, in Jones, "Leo Sowerby: His Life and His Choral Music," 6.

17. Sowerby autobiographical notes, in Hinds, "Leo Sowerby: A Biography," 13.

18. Interview with Nolton, in Hinds, "Leo Sowerby: A Biography," 15.

19. Sowerby autobiographical notes, in Jones, "Leo Sowerby: His Life and His Choral Music," 7.

20. Hinds, "Leo Sowerby: A Biography," 18–19.

21. Sowerby autobiographical notes, in Hinds, "Leo Sowerby: A Biography," 16–17.

22. See, for instance, Tuthill, "Leo Sowerby," 250; Huntington, "A Study of the Musical Contributions of Leo Sowerby," 10–11; Hinds, "Leo Sowerby: A Biography," 17–18; Jones, "Leo Sowerby: His Life and His Choral Music," 5–6; and Kierman, "The Compositions of Leo Sowerby for Organ Solo," 3.

23. Letter dated August 29, 1953, Sowerby autobiographical notes, in Jones, "Leo Sowerby: His Life and His Choral Music," 6.

24. C.E.W., *Music News*, undated, the Leo Sowerby Papers, Special Collections Research Center, Syracuse University Libraries.

25. Maurice Rosenfeld, "'All American' Is Concert at Orchestra Hall," *Chicago Examiner*, November 19, 1913, 8.

26. Adolf Brune, "Mr. Gunn's Orchestral Program of American Music," *Chicago Inter Ocean*, November 19, 1913.

27. E.B.K., "Gunn Conducts Concert of American Music," *Chicago Tribune*, November 19, 1913, 11.

28. For a consideration of d'Indy and arguments against his supposed dislike of Debussy see Brian Hart, "Vincent d'Indy and the Development of the French Symphony," *Music & Letters* 87, no. 2 (2016): 237.

29. Sowerby, letter to the *Chicago Music News*, January 6, 1915.

30. Huntington, "A Study of the Musical Contributions of Leo Sowerby," 12–13.

31. This friendship was evidenced as early as 1914, when Sowerby dedicated his organ *Chorale Prelude on a Melodic Fragment by Palestrina* to "my friend, Eric DeLamarter." DeLamarter soon introduced the piece into his own recital repertory, a work that Harold Milligan called a "striking, even startling, contrast to the sedate old chorale preludes from a by-gone epoch. . . . So modern is Mr. Sowerby that his music belongs to tomorrow, rather than today." See Milligan, "New Music," *The Diapason* 11 (1920): 21.

32. Huntington, "A Study of the Musical Contributions of Leo Sowerby," 15

33. *Chicago Daily Journal*, April 20, 1914.

34. Chicago Symphony Orchestra program, March 11, 1915.

35. Maurice Rosenfeld, "American Concert Is a Big Success," *Musical America*, March 1915.

36. A.H.S., "Prize Symphony Disappoints," unknown source. Cited in Hinds, "Leo Sowerby: A Biography," 31.

37. Letter from Leo Sowerby to Percy Grainger, February 28, 1916. Grainger Museum collection, University of Melbourne.

38. Sowerby reportedly made these comments to his students William Ferris and Ronald Stalford. Conversation with Francis Crociata, April 28, 2022.

39. In a program note penned under the name Richard Brockwell, Powell wrote of his *Rhapsodie*: "In the case of negro music, there is, over and above such qualities as those mentioned, an additional spirit which leads a peculiar and heightened interest. This interest comes from the fact that the negro not merely occupies a subordinate position in the political and social organization of America, but is, au fond, in spite of his surface polish and restraints imposed by close contact with Caucasian civilization, a genuine primitive [. . . .] In addition, to this there is still another stronger characteristic of negro music: The negro is the child among the peoples, and his music shows the unconscious unbound gaiety of the child, as well as the child's humor; sometimes Aesopian, often, unfortunately too often, Rabelaisian."

40. Leo Sowerby, letter to Percy Grainger, March 16, 1924, Grainger Museum collection, University of Melbourne.

41. Sarah Kirby, "Cosmopolitanism and Race in Percy Grainger's American 'Delius Campaign,'" *Current Musicology* 101 (Fall 2017): 39.

42. Leo Sowerby, Letter to Florence Price, April 8, regarding the N.A.A.C.C., Florence Price Papers, University of Arkansas University Libraries, Special Collections.

43. Huntington, "A Study of the Musical Contributions of Leo Sowerby," 17; and Malcolm Halliday, liner notes for *Impressions: Piano Music of Leo Sowerby*, Malcolm Halliday, piano, Albany Records TR226, 1997, compact disc.

44. Grainger, "My Musical Outlook," cited in *Grainger on Music*, ed. Malcolm Gillies and Bruce Clunies Ross (Oxford: Oxford University Press, 1999), 13.

45. Grainger, "The World Music of To-morrow: A Prospect of the Nature of Our Musical Progress Based upon the Musical Tendencies of To-day," *Etude* 34, no. 6 (June 1916): 412. Cited in Gillies and Ross, *Grainger on Music*, 13.

46. Percy Grainger, "Let Us Sit in Wait No Longer for the Advent of Great American Composers—They Are with Us Already," *Quarter-notes of the Brooklyn Music School Settlement*, December 10, 1919, 1–3. Cited in Gillies and Ross, *Grainger on Music*, 108.

47. Robert Rayfield observes that Sowerby suggested this periodization to him in a conversation from 1950. See Rayfield, "A Formal Analysis of the Solo Organ Works of Leo Sowerby to 1960" (DM diss., Northwestern University, 1962), 6.

48. Rayfield, "A Formal Analysis," 7.

49. Felix Borowski, "A Young Composer and His Music," *Chicago Herald*, January 19, 1917; C.E.W., "Music in Chicago," *Music News*, January 1917; Maurice Rosenfeld, "Chicago Concerts of Notable Worth," *Musical America*, January 27, 1917, 42.

50. Farnsworth Wright, "One Great Composer Our Need in America, Urges DeLamarter," *Musical America*, February 3, 1917, 35.

51. Sowerby, letter to Grainger, October 11, 1918, Grainger Museum collection, University of Melbourne.

52. Sowerby, letter to Grainger, November 19, 1918, Grainger Museum collection, University of Melbourne.

53. Sowerby, letter to Daniel Gregory Mason, February 28, 1918. Daniel Gregory Mason Papers, Columbia University Libraries, Archival Collections.

54. I am grateful to Francis Crociata for providing this insight.

55. Henriette Weber, "Sowerby in Fourfold Success," *Chicago Examiner*, February 16, 1918; and Edward C. Moore, "Noted Cellist Is Heard with the Orchestra," *Chicago Journal*, February 16, 1918.

56. Frederick Donaghey, "The Orchestra's Nineteenth," *Chicago Daily Tribune*, February 16, 1918, II/7; and Felix Borowski, "The Symphony Concert," *Chicago Herald*, February 16, 1918.

57. Charles A. Quitzow, "Sowerby Agitates San Franciscans," *Musical America*, December 2, 1922.

58. Sowerby, letter to Percy and Rose Grainger, February 18, 1919, Grainger Museum collection, University of Melbourne.

59. Sowerby conversation with Kierman, in Kierman, "The Compositions of Leo Sowerby for Organ Solo," 7.

## Chapter 2. Home and Away (1919–27)

1. "News and Notes: A New Season for the Orchestras," *New York Times*, October 14, 1917.

2. Horowitz, *Classical Music in America: A History of Its Rise and Fall*, 269.

3. Oja, "Forging an International Alliance," 196.

4. *The Congregationalist and Christian World*, December 13, 1919, 864.

5. *New Music Review* 20 (1920): 67.

6. For more on Skinner's innovations see Stotler, "The Influence of the American Orchestral Organ on Selected Works of Leo Sowerby," 7–10.

7. For more on Coolidge's biography and patronage history see Oja, "Forging an International Alliance," 196–98.

8. "New Piece Given at Second Concert," *Berkshire Evening Eagle*, September 26, 1919.

9. Daniel Gregory Mason, "The Berkshire Festival of Chamber Music," unidentified publication from the scrapbook of Bertha Wiersma Nolton, November 1919, in Hinds, "Leo Sowerby: A Biography," 62.

10. This correspondence survives as part of the Daniel Gregory Mason Papers, Columbia University Libraries, Archival Collections.

11. W. L. Hubbard, "America Will Lose Its Greatest Composer If Sowerby Goes Abroad," *Chicago Daily Tribune*, March 6, 1920.

12. Sowerby, letter to Coolidge, March 16, 1920, Elizabeth Sprague Coolidge Foundation Collection, Music Division, Library of Congress.

13. "Sowerby's 'Comes Autumn Time,' a Brilliant Musical Expression," *Musical America*, March 20, 1920.

14. Huntington leaves the source of this anecdote open, though Tuthill attributes the remark to Sonneck. See Huntington, "A Study of the Musical Contributions of Leo Sowerby," 26; and Tuthill, "Leo Sowerby," 249.

15. Margie A. McLeod, "Apathy Drawing Us Back under Foreign Domination, Says Sowerby," *Musical America*, February 12, 1921, 15.

16. D'Indy, letter to Sowerby, January 11, 1919, Leo Sowerby Papers, Special Collections Research Center, Syracuse University Libraries.

17. For a detailed history of the Rome Prize see Olmstead, "The Rome Prize from Leo Sowerby to David Diamond," 13–41.

18. Oja, "Forging an International Alliance," 195–221.

19. For a detailed description of these letters and of Sowerby's broader activities in Rome, with an emphasis on Coolidge's involvement, see Oja, "Forging an International Alliance," 203–12.

20. For a listing of Sowerby performances during this period see Oja, "Forging an International Alliance," 212–14.

21. Karleton Hackett, "Leo Sowerby Reaps Honors in Europe Tour," *Chicago Evening Post*, September 13, 1922.

22. Edwin Evans, "The Salzburg Festival," *Musical Times* 63, no. 955 (1922): 628. Evans called the sonata "a well-written but not overwhelmingly original example, finely played by an Italian violist, Mario Corti, and the composer."

23. David Cooper, *Béla Bartók* (New Haven, CT: Yale University Press, 2015), 182 and 184.

24. Felix Lamond, "Report of the Professor of Musical Composition: To the Trustees of the American Academy in Rome, for the year ending September 30, 1923," 50.

25. Florence French, ed., "Chicago Composer on Symphony Program," *Musical Leader* 43 (April 13, 1922): 367.

26. Felix Borowski, "Mr. Sowerby's Symphony," *Boston Evening Transcript*, April 13, 1922.

27. Sowerby, letter to Coolidge, November 2, [1921], Elizabeth Sprague Coolidge Foundation Collection, Music Division, Library of Congress.

28. Edgar Ansel Mowrer, "Americans in Rome Fellows in Academy; Leo Sowerby a Central Figure in Music; His Compatriots Win Honors," *Chicago Daily News*, February 3, 1923.

29. Maurice Rosenfeld, "First Grand Prize in Music to Sowerby; Judges in *The Daily News* Contest Unanimous in Choosing Chicagoan's Work," *Chicago Daily News*, January 28, 1924.

30. Southworth Alden, untitled article, *Minneapolis Daily Star*, January 9, 1926.

31. DeLamarter, letter to Sowerby, undated, Leo Sowerby Papers, Special Collections Research Center, Syracuse University Libraries.

32. Ronald Huntington, ed., *Psalm Oratorio by Leo Sowerby* (Chicago: Leo Sowerby Foundation, 1993), preface.

33. The performance, led by Robert Hobgood (a doctoral candidate at the time), is an arranged version of the first movement and several excerpts from later movements for organ, brass, and percussion.

34. Northrup, letter to Kahn, December 2, 1924, Leo Sowerby Papers, Special Collections Research Center, Syracuse University Libraries.

35. Northrup, letter to the editor, *New York Telegram and Evening Mail*, December 24, 1924, Leo Sowerby Papers, Special Collections Research Center, Syracuse University Libraries.

36. Northrup, letter to the editor, *New York Telegram and Evening Mail.*

37. *Chicago Daily Journal*, October 12, 1925.

38. Sowerby conversation with Kierman. Cited in Kierman, "The Compositions of Leo Sowerby for Organ Solo," 11.

39. Sowerby autobiographical notes, in Hinds, "Leo Sowerby: A Biography," 91.

40. Huntington, liner notes for *Leo Sowerby: Works for Organ and Orchestra*, David Craighead, David Mulbury, organ, Fairfield Orchestra, John Welsh, conductor, Naxos 8.559028, 1999, compact disc.

41. Huntington, liner notes for *Leo Sowerby: Works for Organ and Orchestra.*

42. Douglas Shadle, *Antonín Dvořák's New World Symphony* (Oxford: Oxford University Press, 2021), 74–75.

43. These issues are thoroughly treated in Shadle, *Antonín Dvořák's New World Symphony.*

44. Sowerby, "The Folk-Element—The Vitalizer of Modern Music," *Musical Scrap Book Magazine* 1, no. 1 (1927): 1–2, 11.

45. Sowerby, "The Folk-Element," 1.

46. Sowerby, "The Folk-Element," 11.

47. Levy, *Frontier Figures: American Music and the Mythology of the American West*, 167–68.

48. Sowerby, "The Folk-Element," 11.

49. Sowerby, "The Folk-Element," cited in Huntington, "A Study of the Musical Contributions of Leo Sowerby," 200 and 202.

50. Dena J. Epstein, "Frederick Stock and American Music," *American Music* 10, no. 1 (1992): 23.

51. Alfred V. Frankenstein, "Twenty-five Years a Conductor," *Review of Reviews* (New York) 81 (January 1930): 96.

52. Howard Hanson, "Report of the Committee on American Music," Music Teachers' National Association, *Proceedings* 33 (1938): 330–34, quoted in Epstein, "Frederick Stock and American Music," 31.

53. Quoted in Howard Pollack, *John Alden Carpenter* (Urbana: University of Illinois Press, 1995), 154.

54. Pollack, *John Alden Carpenter*, 391; and John Alden Carpenter, letter to Leo Sowerby, May 7, 1946, Leo Sowerby Papers, Special Collections Research Center, Syracuse University Libraries.

55. Samantha Ege, "Chicago, the 'City We Love to Call Home!': Intersectionality, Narrativity, and Locale in the Music of Florence Beatrice Price and Theodora Sturkow Ryder," *American Music* 39, no. 1 (2021): 1–40.

56. "Evanti Praises Woman Composer: Florence B. Price Lauded by Concert Star," *Pittsburgh Courier*, October 13, 1934, 9. Quoted in Ege, "Chicago, the 'City We Love to Call Home!'" 6; and Ege, "Composing a Symphonist: Florence Price and the Hand of Black Women's Fellowship," *Women and Music: A Journal of Gender and Culture* 24 (2020): 7–27.

57. Oja, *Making Music Modern*, 361.

58. Henry Taylor Parker, untitled article, *Boston Evening Transcript*, March 12, 1932.

59. Paul Rosenfeld, "Musical Chronicle," *The Dial*, December 1924, 532.

*Chapter 3. The Church Ascendant (1927–40)*

1. Edward Dickinson, *Music in the History of the Western Church* (New York: Haskell House, 1902), 390.

2. For a useful survey of these developments see Ogasapian, *Church Music in America*, 228–51.

3. Paul Henry Lang, "Editorial," *Musical Quarterly* 31 (1945): 517.

4. For more on the history of the American Guild of Organists see Agnes Armstrong, "American Guild of Organists Centennial: The Examinations and Academic Regalia of the American Guild of Organists," *American Organist* 30, no. 7 (1996): 44–55.

5. Ogasapian, *Church Music in America*, 234.

6. Rima Lunin Schultz, *The Church and the City: A Social History of 150 Years at Saint James, Chicago* (Chicago: Cathedral of Saint James, 1986), 187–89.

7. Schultz, *The Church and the City*, 187.

8. Stephen Buzard, "Leo Sowerby: His Life, Work, and Theology of Church Music," *Journal of the Association of Anglican Musicians* 27 (2018): 4; and Huntington, "A Study of the Musical Contributions of Leo Sowerby," 34.

9. Letter from Reverend Duncan Browne to Sowerby, March 4, 1927, Leo Sowerby Foundation, Kilgore, TX.

10. Schultz, *The Church and the City*, 190–92.

11. Leo Sowerby, "Leading Composer Writes of Changed Standards," *The Diapason* 51 (1959): 45.

12. Lester W. Groom, "Chicago," *American Organist* 11 (1928): 260.

13. Sowerby, "A Good Creed," *American Organist* 12 (1929): 223.

14. A letter from Herbert Howells to Sowerby describes Howells's sadness upon learning that Sowerby would be returning to America ("Does this mean your Rome days are at an end? And your excursions to London a thing of the past? More's the pity if it is so.") and his vow to share his own music with Sowerby, with the rejoinder that "You must retaliate by hurling things of yours at *me*." Howells, letter to Sowerby, August 18, 1924, Leo Sowerby Papers, Special Collections Research Center, Syracuse University Libraries.

15. See Jones, "Leo Sowerby: His Life and His Choral Music," 551–81.

16. Buzard, "Leo Sowerby," 5.

17. Jones, "Leo Sowerby: His Life and His Choral Music," 107; and Huntington, "A Study of the Musical Contributions of Leo Sowerby," 34.

18. Madeleine Goss, *Modern Music Makers* (New York: E. P. Dutton, 1952), 126.

19. Sowerby, "Music at St. James'," *Diocese of Chicago* 10 (October 1934): 39.

20. A selective list of anthems of this type include "Now There Lightens upon Us" (1935, for a boys choir concert sponsored by the Chicago Choirmasters' Association); "O Light, from Age to Age" (1936, sixty-fifth anniversary of Chicago's Fourth Presbyterian Church); "O Jesu, Thou the Beauty Art" (1938, for Carlton Borrow and the English Boy

Choristers, of the London Choir School); "Blessed Are All They That Fear the Lord" (1939, fiftieth anniversary of Reverend Duncan Browne's tenure as rector of Saint James); Psalm 122 (1941, for Washington Cathedral and dedicated to Henry St. George Tucker, presiding bishop of the Episcopal Church); "Come, Holy Ghost" (1949, commissioned by Washington Cathedral for 400th anniversary of the Book of Common Prayer); "The Armor of God" (1951, for the choir of Saint Paul's School in Concord, NH); "Come Ye, and Let Us Go Up" (1952, 100th anniversary of Grace Episcopal Church, Saint Luke's Hospital Chapel); and "I Will Love Thee, O Lord" (published 1956, for the choir of Saint George's Cathedral, Kingston, Ontario, Canada).

21. With respect to Sowerby's anthems, Terry Fansler has observed that all-Sowerby programs appeared frequently at meetings of the American Guild of Organists and of choral directors' associations in the 1930s and 1940s, but that "the greatest influence of this composer has been somewhat contained within the Episcopal church." See Fansler, "The Anthem in America: 1900–1950" (PhD diss., North Texas State University, 1982), 74.

22. Ogasapian, *Church Music in America*, 245.

23. Robert Rayfield, "Leo Sowerby," *Music: The A.G.O. and R.C.C.O Magazine* 10, no. 11 (1976): 40.

24. Personal letters from Stella Roberts (October 1970), B. G. Gross (November 2, 1970), and Marion Schroeder Levitt (November 27, 1970). Cited in Hinds, "Leo Sowerby," 93.

25. H. L. Morrow, "Leo Sowerby and His Work for American Church Music," *Musical Times* 73, no. 1074 (1932): 734.

26. Personal letter from Anne Douglas. Cited in Jones, "Leo Sowerby: His Life and His Choral Music," 165.

27. Personal letter from Anne Douglas. Cited in Jones, "Leo Sowerby: His Life and His Choral Music," 166.

28. Unpublished diary, the Leo Sowerby Foundation, Kilgore, TX. The comments on Sowerby's personal tastes come from interviews with Ronald Stalford and Bertha Nolton in Hinds, "Leo Sowerby," 102.

29. Personal conversation with Francis Crociata, April 28, 2022.

30. Personal conversation with Francis Crociata, April 28, 2022.

31. The information in the following several paragraphs is derived largely from a personal conversation with Francis Crociata, April 28, 2022.

32. Ned Rorem, *Knowing When to Stop* (New York: Simon and Schuster, 1994), 139–40.

33. When asked why he had not composed any organ music during this period, Sowerby offered the pithy reply that he simply had no desire to do so. See Rayfield, "A Formal Analysis," 29.

34. Rayfield, "A Formal Analysis," 29–30; and Rayfield, "Leo Sowerby," 41.

35. For more on the specifications of these organs see Stotler, "The Influence of the American Orchestral Organ," 5–10.

36. For more on these style periods see Rayfield, "A Formal Analysis"; Stolter, "The Influence of the American Orchestral Organ," 11–42; and Rayfield, liner notes to *Sowerby at Trinity*.

37. Among these studies are Rayfield, "A Formal Analysis"; Kierman, "The Compositions of Leo Sowerby for Organ Solo"; Margaret Mitchell, "Leo Sowerby's Solo Organ Compositions Based on Hymn Tunes" (MM thesis, North Texas State University, 1966);

Edwin Rieke, "The Organ Choral Preludes of Leo Sowerby" (DMA diss., Eastman School of Music, 1975); Robert Parris, "A Performer's Companion to Leo Sowerby's *Symphony in G Major* for Organ" (DMA diss., Eastman School of Music, 1982); and Stolter, "The Influence of the American Orchestral Organ." Other studies that analyze one or more Sowerby works include Parks, "A Critical Analysis of the Works of Leo Sowerby," 25–55; Huntington, "A Study of the Musical Contributions of Leo Sowerby," 70–156; Richard Beckford, "The Organ Symphony: Its Evolution in France and Transformation in Selected Works by American Composers of the Twentieth Century" (DMA diss., Louisiana State University, 1997), 30–40; and Sarah Read-Gehrenbeck, "'Why Should the Devil Have All the Pretty Tunes?' The Great Awakening of a New American Idiom: Organ Music Based on Shape-Note Hymns" (DM diss., Indiana University, 2017), 51–53.

38. The following summary derives mostly from Rayfield, "A Formal Analysis," 4–6.

39. William Lester, "New Music," *The Diapason* 23 (October 1932): 15.

40. See for instance Huntington, "A Study of the Musical Contributions of Leo Sowerby," 104–22; Rayfield, "A Formal Analysis," 33–45; Lucile Hammill Webb, "A Study of the G Major Symphony for Organ by Leo Sowerby" (MM thesis, Eastman School of Music, 1945); Parris, "A Performer's Companion"; and Beckford, "The Organ Symphony," 34–40.

41. Arnold Schoenberg, "Criteria for the Evaluation of Music," in *Style and Idea: Selected Writings of Arnold Schoenberg*, ed. Leonard Stein (Berkeley and Los Angeles: University of California Press, 1975), 129.

42. This anecdote appears in several sources, a recent example of which is an *Examiner Live* article from 2013 featuring organist Gordon Stewart. See "Kirklees Organist Gordon Stewart Plays World's Toughest Piece of Organ Music," *Examiner Live*, July 12, 2013, accessed March 16, 2019, https://www.examinerlive.co.uk/news/west-yorkshire-news/kirklees-organist-gordon-stewart-plays-4959569.

43. Huntington, "A Study of the Musical Contributions of Leo Sowerby," 123.

44. Rayfield, "A Formal Analysis," 30–31.

45. E. Power Biggs, "Koussevitzky and Concert Hall Organs," *American Organist* 12, no. 3 (March 1978): 28–29.

46. Owen, *E. Power Biggs: Concert Organist*, 58.

47. Owen, *E. Power Biggs, Concert Organist*, 152.

48. Personal conversation with Francis Crociata, April 28, 2022.

49. Letter from Jim Gray to Sowerby, June 24, 1941, Leo Sowerby Papers, Special Collections Research Center, Syracuse University Libraries.

50. T. Scott Buhrman, "Repertoire and Reviews," *American Organist* 24 (1941): 102.

51. Leonard M. Ellinwood, program notes to premiere performance of *The Throne of God* at Washington Cathedral, with the Washington and Cathedral Choral Societies, November 18, 1957.

52. The only extensive scholarly writing on this piece to date, a 1956 master's thesis by V. Lee Stallings, similarly privileges harmony as the cantata's most distinctive element. Stallings's study is organized around strictly musical elements (melody, rhythm, counterpoint, harmony, form); its cataloging of various devices offers a valuable assemblage of materials and offers some thoughts about the relative importance of each element, as well as certain stylistic comparisons to other Sowerby sacred works. See Stallings, "A Study of *Forsaken of Man*, a Sacred Cantata by Leo Sowerby" (MSM thesis, Southern Baptist Theological

Seminary, 1956), 99. For an exhaustive catalog of various types of tonal sonorities see Stallings, "A Study of *Forsaken of Man*," 40–50.

53. Crociata, liner notes to *Leo Sowerby: Symphony No. 2*.

54. In program notes that accompanied Chicago Symphony performances of this work in the 1950s and 1960s, Sowerby observed: "It may be added that while the classic design of the Passacaglia has been adhered to rather strictly, the entire conception of the music is unacademic, and if anything, romantic." Cited in Crociata, liner notes to *Leo Sowerby: Symphony No. 2*.

55. Biggs, unpublished notes. Cited in Owen, *E. Power Biggs, Concert Organist*, 50.

56. "Sowerby, Greatest of American Composers," *Colorado Springs Gazette and Telegraph*, February 6, 1935.

57. Cited in Eugene Stinson, "Music Views," *Chicago News*, undated clipping.

58. Cited in Crociata, liner notes to *Leo Sowerby: Symphony No. 2*.

59. Many of the following details appear in Sowerby's own notes to this piece, as published in Crociata, liner notes to *Leo Sowerby: Symphony No. 2*.

60. Jones, "Leo Sowerby: His Life and His Choral Music," 93–95.

61. "Virtual Museum Exhibit at Carl Sandburg Home National Historic Site," accessed March 11, 2020, https://www.nps.gov/museum/exhibits/carl/visionary.html.

62. Carl Sandburg, *The American Songbag* (New York: Harcourt, Brace, 1927), x.

63. Levy, *Frontier Figures*, 161.

64. Levy, *Frontier Figures*, 160–68.

65. Tuthill, "Leo Sowerby," 252–53.

66. Glenn Dillard Gunn, untitled article, *Chicago Herald and Examiner*, March 21, 1931.

67. James Davies, untitled article, *Minneapolis Tribune*, March 18, 1933.

68. Philip Hale, "Sowerby's 'Prairie,'" *Boston Herald*, March 12, 1932.

69. *Time*, April 10, 1933, 28.

70. Interview with Ronald Stalford, Washington DC, July 2, 1970. Cited in Hinds, "Leo Sowerby," 99–100.

71. E. Power Biggs, unpublished notes. Cited in Owen, *E. Power Biggs, Concert Organist*, 50.

72. Personal letters from Roberts (October 1970), Gross (November 2, 1970), and Paul Callaway (December 1970). Cited in Hinds, "Leo Sowerby," 99.

73. Francis Crociata, liner notes for *Corridors of Light: Music of William Ferris*, William Ferris Chorale, William Ferris, conductor, Cedille Records CDR 7004, 2010, compact disc, 7.

74. "Leo Sowerby: A Symposium of Tribute," 27.

75. Rae Linda Brown, *The Heart of a Woman: The Life and Music of Florence B. Price* (Urbana: University of Illinois Press, 2020), 145.

76. Rorem, *Knowing When to Stop*, 140.

*Chapter 4. Secular Decline, Sacred Rise (1940–62)*

1. Emily Abrams Ansari, *The Sound of a Superpower: Musical Americanism and the Cold War* (Oxford: Oxford University Press, 2018), 16–21.

2. Ansari, *The Sound of a Superpower*, 21.

3. Ansari, *The Sound of a Superpower*, 7.

4. Interview with Stephen Buzard, October 13, 2021.

5. "Portrait of a Great Man—Leo Sowerby," *Showcase: Music Clubs Magazine* 40, no. 1 (September–October 1960): 10.

6. These include former Sowerby student and American Conservatory faculty member Maude Ogle, who premiered the initial 1948 version; Gail Quillman, who performed and made the first recording of a revised version with several cuts; and what Sowerby considered the "true" premiere of the final version, by Grace Weiser in February 1964 at the Library of Congress. Personal conversation with Francis Crociata, April 28, 2022.

7. Douglas Shadle, *Orchestrating the Nation: The Nineteenth-Century American Symphonic Enterprise* (Oxford: Oxford University Press, 2016).

8. Nicholas Tawa, *The Great American Symphony: Music, the Depression, and War* (Bloomington and Indianapolis: Indiana University Press, 2009), 1–3.

9. Eugene Goossens, letter to Sowerby, December 21, 1942, Leo Sowerby Papers, Special Collections Research Center, Syracuse University Libraries.

10. Correspondence between Sowerby and Koussevitzky, September 25 and 28, 1940, Serge Koussevitzky Archive, 1920–76, Music Division, Library of Congress.

11. Charles Quint, "Stock Introduces New Sowerby Work," *Musical America*, March 25, 1941, 22.

12. Remi Gassmann, "Jubilee Wind-Up," *Modern Music* 18 (1941): 264.

13. Letter to Richard Weagly, June 27, 1949, Seth Bingham Archives, New York Public Library at Lincoln Center; and Searle Wright, "Seth Daniels Bingham: 100th Anniversary," *American Organist* 16, no. 6 (June 1982): 40–44.

14. For a detailed analysis of this piece see Sargent, "Forgetting and Remembering," 485–517.

15. See, for instance, Stephen Walsh, "Stravinsky's Choral Music," *Tempo* 81 (1967): 44–45; Rose A. Zak, "Dialogue and Discourse in Stravinsky's 'Symphony of Psalms,'" *Criticism* 22, no. 4 (Fall 1980): 357–75; Richard Taruskin, *Stravinsky and the Russian Traditions: A Biography of the Works through Mavra* (Oxford: Oxford University Press, 1996), 1618; Per Dahl, "Text, Identity, and Belief in Stravinsky's Symphony of Psalms," *Danish Musicology Online*, special edition (2016): 61–80; and Barbara Heyman, *Samuel Barber: The Composer and His Music*, 2nd ed. (New York: Oxford University Press, 2020), 385–96.

16. Biggs, personal letter, March 8, 1971. Cited in Hinds, "Leo Sowerby," 97–98.

17. Quoted in John von Rhein, "Belated Amends," *Chicago Tribune*, May 4, 1990, https://www.chicagotribune.com/news/ct-xpm-1990-05-04-9002060742-story.html.

18. Jim Gray, telegram to Leo Sowerby, May 7, 1946, Leo Sowerby Papers, Special Collections Research Center, Syracuse University Libraries.

19. Charles Buckley, "Hails Creative Genius of Modest Leo Sowerby," *Chicago Herald-American*, November 2, 1952, 4.

20. Personal conversation with Francis Crociata, April 28, 2022.

21. Glenn Dillard Gunn, untitled article, *Washington D.C. Times-Herald*, May 24, 1953.

22. Samuel Barber, letter to Leo Sowerby, October 15, 1954, Leo Sowerby Papers, Special Collections Research Center, Syracuse University Libraries.

23. Warren Martin, "Three American Composers: Clokey, Sowerby, Lockwood," *Repertoire* 1, no. 2 (November 1951): 114–15.

24. Howard Hanson, *Music in Contemporary Civilization* (Lincoln: University of Nebraska Press, 1951), 16–17.

25. Leo Sowerby: A Symposium of Tribute," 64.

26. Aaron Copland, "Our Younger Generation—Ten Years Later," *Modern Music* 13, no. 4 (May–June 1936): 4.

27. Conversation with Francis Crociata, April 28, 2022.

28. For an assessment of Thomson's criticism during this period see Tim Page, *Virgil Thomson: Music Chronicles 1940–54* (New York: Library of America, 2014).

29. Cecil Smith, "Sowerby's New Work Will Be Given Premiere," *Chicago Daily Tribune*, March 2?, 1941.

30. Program notes, "Two Organ Recitals Commemorating the Centenary of the Birth of Leo Sowerby (1895–1968), Saint Thomas Church, April 23 & 40, 1995," the Leo Sowerby Foundation, Kilgore, TX.

31. Carol Doran, "Popular Religious Song," in *The Hymnal 1982 Companion*, ed. Raymond F. Glover (New York: Church Hymnal Corporation, 1990), 13–28.

32. Sowerby, *Ideals in Church Music: An Official Statement Prepared for the Joint Commission on Church Music of the Protestant Episcopal Church in the United States of America* (Greenwich, CT: Seabury Press, 1956), 5–6.

33. Doran, "Popular Religious Song," 22.

34. Paul Callaway, letter to the Rev. Howard S. Kennedy, April 23, 1952, the Leo Sowerby Foundation, Kilgore, TX.

35. Seth Bingham, letter to Leo Sowerby, April 18, 1952, the Leo Sowerby Foundation, Kilgore, TX.

36. Leonard Ellinwood, letter to Leo Sowerby, April 13, 1952, the Leo Sowerby Foundation, Kilgore, TX.

37. Talmage W. Dean, *A Survey of Twentieth Century Protestant Church Music in America* (Nashville, TN: Boardman Press, 1988), 193.

38. Sowerby, "Church Musician Duties Defined in CCO Lecture," *The Diapason* 50, no. 1 (1958): 8, 40–41. The original speech was delivered on August 27, 1958, at the Canadian College of Organists convention in Ottawa.

39. Sowerby, "Church Musician Duties Defined," 40.

40. See "Sowerby Paper and Works Heard by Van Dusen Club," *The Diapason* 32 (March 1941): 4; "Sowerby's Faith and Works," *The Diapason* 34 (July 1943): 2; and Jones, "Leo Sowerby: His Life and His Choral Music," 177–78.

41. Sowerby, *Ideals in Church Music*. The joint commission, first established in 1919, was charged with establishing recommendations for the "character and for of music to be used in the services of the church, and in the schools and colleges, together with methods of instruction in theological schools in the history and practice of Church Music." It produced regular reports on matters of church music repertory and standards of quality. For more on the commission see G. Edward Stubbs, "Ecclesiastical Music," *New Music Review and Church Music Review* 21, no. 241 (December 1921): 417.

42. Dean, *A Survey of Twentieth Century Protestant Church Music*, 194.

43. Sowerby, *Ideals in Church Music*, 5.

44. Here Sowerby specifically cites masses by Haydn, Mozart, Gioachino Rossini, and Charles Gounod, which he calls "unchurchly."

45. Sowerby, *Ideals in Church Music*, 17.

46. Sowerby, "Composition in Relation to the Church and Allied Fields in America," in *Organ and Choral Aspects and Prospects*, ed. Max Hinrichsen (London: Hinrichsen Edition, 1958), 33–46.

47. Sowerby, "Composition in Relation to the Church," 33–34.

48. Sowerby, "Composition in Relation to the Church," 34.

49. Sowerby, "Church Musician Duties Defined in CCO Lecture," 8, 40–41.

50. Sowerby, "Church Musician Duties Defined in CCO Lecture," 8.

51. Sowerby, "Church Musician Duties Defined in CCO Lecture," 40.

52. Sowerby, "The Compleat Choirmaster" (unpublished manuscript, 1961), 1, the Leo Sowerby Papers, Special Collections Research Center, Syracuse University Libraries.

53. Sowerby, "The Compleat Choirmaster," 1.

54. Ogasapian, *Church Music in America*, 228–51. The following summary of trends is drawn largely from Ogasapian's survey, as well as Alec Wyton, "Twentieth Century American Church Music," in *Duty and Delight: Routley Remembered: A Memorial Tribute to Erik Routley (1917–1982)*, ed. Robin A. Leaver, James H. Litton, and Carlton R. Young (Carol Stream, IL: Hope Publishing Company, 1985), 79–88.

55. Erik Routley, *Twentieth-Century Church Music*, rev. ed. (London: Herbert Jenkins, 1966), 88.

56. Sowerby, *Ideals in Church Music*, 15.

57. Sowerby, *Ideals in Church Music*, 15.

58. Sowerby, *Ideals in Church Music*, 15.

59. Sowerby, *Ideals in Church Music*, 12.

60. Sowerby, *Ideals in Church Music*, 12.

61. Sowerby, "Composition in Relation to the Church," 33–34.

62. Sowerby, "The Compleat Choirmaster," 1.

63. David McK. Williams, "The Modernist in Church Music: An Address" (New York: Hymn Society, 1935).

64. Sowerby, "The Compleat Choirmaster," 5–6.

65. Alan Rich, "Our Changing Music," *New York Herald Tribune*, October 2, 1963, 19.

66. Glenn Dillard Gunn, "Sowerby Pieces Mystify Hearers at Organ Recital," *Washington Times-Herald*, February 24, 1949; and Paul Hume, "Unrestrained Applause Honors Composer," *Washington Post*, November 19, 1957, B1.

*Chapter 5. Washington and the College of Church Musicians (1962–68)*

1. "The Report of a Colloquium on the Training of Church Musicians," *Cathedral Age* (Summer 1953): 12–13.

2. Neill Phillips, "A Proposed College of Church Musicians," *Cathedral Age* (Fall 1961): 38–39.

3. "Income of Families and Persons in the United States: 1962," United States Census Bureau Report Number P60–41, October 21, 1963, https://www.census.gov/library/publications/1963/demo/p60-041.html.

4. Donal J. Henahan, "Leo Sowerby, Director, College of Church Musicians," *Cathedral Age* (Fall 1963): 6.

5. Letters from Leo Sowerby to William Ferris, Leo Sowerby Papers, Northwestern University. All quotations in the following paragraph are taken from these letters.

6. Francis B. Sayre Jr., "Sermon Preached in Washington Cathedral, September 16, 1962," Leo Sowerby Papers, Special Collections Research Center, Syracuse University Libraries.

7. Interview with Pat Partridge, February 27, 2021.

8. Letter from Preston Rockholt, September 1, 1971. Cited in Jones, "Leo Sowerby: His Life and His Choral Music," 235; and letter to William Ferris, January 28, 1965, Leo Sowerby Papers, Northwestern University.

9. Interview with Stalford, in Hinds, "Leo Sowerby: A Biography," 119.

10. Letter from Eugene Ormandy to Leo Sowerby, December 14, 1964, the Leo Sowerby Foundation, Kilgore, TX.

11. The committee for the Koussevitzky grant included the conductor's widow Olga Koussevitzky, along with Leonard Bernstein, Aaron Copland, and Ed Waters, chief of the Library of Congress's music division. While perusing the candidate list Waters reportedly asked, "What about Sowerby?" to which Bernstein (who never conducted Sowerby's music) pithily responded, "He's still alive?" Crociata suggests that the decision to grant Sowerby the award was somewhat politically motived by a desire to keep Waters happy. Personal conversation with Crociata, April 28, 2022.

12. Francis B. Sayre Jr., "Sermon, Preached at the Memorial Service for Leo Sowerby Held at St. Thomas Church, New York City, October 27, 1968," *Journal of Church Music* 11 (June 1969): 6.


## Epilogue

1. Lawrence Sears, "Leo Sowerby Had a Varied and Interesting Career," *Washington Evening Star*, October 12, 1968.

2. Interview with Stephen Buzard, October 13, 2021. The following quotes from Buzard are all taken from the same interview.

3. The roundtable featured William Ferris, moderator; Richard Carter, Esther LaBerge Ganz, Leo Heim, Robert Lind, Marion Schrader, and Ronald Stalford.

4. "A Sowerby Celebration," Cedille Records, accessed March 3, 2021, https://www.cedillerecords.org/a-sowerby-celebration.

5. Interview with Jim Ginsburg, March 21, 2021.

## Organ Music

*Arioso*   *Leo Sowerby: Works for Organ.* Lorenz Maycher, organ. Raven Records OAR-310, 1995, compact disc. https://www.youtube.com/watch?v=TXRt7IZVHM8.

*Comes Autumn Time*   *Organ Music by Frank Ferko & Leo Sowerby.* David Schrader, organ. Cedille Records CDR 90000 204, compact disc, 2021. https://www.youtube.com/watch?v=7UJUuoHcEMU.

*Pageant*   *Sowerby at Trinity.* Faythe Freese, organ. Bobby Lewis, trumpet and flugelhorn. Albany Records Troy 368, compact disc, 1999. https://www.youtube.com/watch?v=14T7WkNjCds.

Symphony in G Major for Organ   *Organ Music of Leo Sowerby.* Catharine Crozier, organ. Delos D 3075, compact disc, 1988. https://www.youtube.com/watch?v=MUNMoF9bOrs.

## Choral Music with Organ

*Magnificat and Nunc dimittis in E Major*   *Praise the Lord: Music from St. Thomas's, Fifth Avenue.* Choir of St. Thomas Church, Gerre Hancock, director, Judith Hancock, organ. Argo 425 800–2, compact disc, 1990. https://www.youtube.com/watch?v=hRLrvL-_iRE.

"Now There Lightens Upon Us" and other works   *Love Came Down at Christmas: The Christmas Music of Leo Sowerby.* Convivium, John Delorey and Patricia Snyder, conductors, Patricia Snyder and Ronald Stalford, organ. Albany Records Troy 187, compact disc, 1995. https://www.youtube.com/watch?v=dWiyPg_3GiQ.

Psalm 122 ("I Was Glad When They Said unto Me")   *Choral Music of Leo Sowerby, Vol. 3.* Trinity Church Choir. Gothic Records, compact disc, 1995. https://www.youtube.com/watch?v=umpU6V5i4I8 (YouTube recording by Washington National Cathedral Choir of Men and Girls).

## Orchestral and Jazz

*The Canticle of the* Sun   The *Pulitzer Project: Pulitzer Prize—Winning Works by Schuman, Sowerby & Copland.* Grant Park Chorus & Orchestra, Carlos Kalmar, conductor.

*Suggested Listening*

Cedille Records CDR 90000 125, compact disc, 2011. https://www.youtube.com/watch?v=P1yxjhfSH4A.

*Prairie*   *Prairie: Tone Poems by Leo Sowerby*. Czech National Symphony Orchestra, Paul Freeman, conductor. Cedille Records CDR 90000 033, compact disc, 1997. https://www.youtube.com/watch?v=UWIZ9hcgPko.

Symphony No. 2   *Symphony No. 2 & Other Works*. Chicago Sinfonietta, Czech National Symphony Orchestra, Paul Freeman, conductor. Cedille Records CDR 90000 039, compact disc, 1998. https://www.youtube.com/watch?v=4CiOZ39j9xM&list=OLAK5uy_meTIwkm1N3g9iiStfv2w2AegfAUWvTslY&index=4.

*Synconata*   *The Paul Whiteman Commissions & Other Early Works*. Andy Baker Orchestra, Andy Baker, conductor; Avalon String Quartet; Winston Choi, piano; Alexander Hanna, double bass. Cedille Records CDR 90000 205, compact disc, 2021. https://www.youtube.com/watch?v=ADasrrGwDLw.


*Keyboard and Chamber Music*

*From the Northland: Impressions of Lake Superior County*   *Impressions: Music for Piano by Leo Sowerby*. Malcolm Halliday, piano. Albany TROY226, compact disc, 2000. https://www.youtube.com/watch?v=GQe65Nw7jJI.

Sonata (No. 3) in D for piano   *Leo Sowerby: Piano Works*. Gail Quillman, piano. New World 80376, compact disc, 2007. https://www.youtube.com/watch?v=gmdUqscDFPU.

Trio (No. 3) for violin, violoncello, and piano   *Trios from the City of Big Shoulders*. Lincoln Trio. Cedille Records CDR 90000 203, compact disc, 2021. https://www.youtube.com/watch?v=XRPYW_TWeMI.


*Further Listening*

Other recordings available at the Leo Sowerby Foundation. *YouTube*. https://www.youtube.com/@theleosowerbyfoundation9161.

# SELECTED BIBLIOGRAPHY

Reviews are only cited if they are of substantial length or particular relevance. In addition to the material cited, major sources for this book include scores, manuscripts, papers, correspondence, notebooks, photographs, and other primary sources housed at the Daniel Gregory Mason Papers, Columbia University Libraries, Archival Collections; the Elizabeth Sprague Coolidge Foundation Collection, Music Division, Library of Congress; the Florence Price Papers, University of Arkansas University Libraries, Special Collections; the Grainger Museum collection, University of Melbourne; the Leo Sowerby Foundation, Kilgore, Texas; the Leo Sowerby Papers, Northwestern University; the Leo Sowerby Papers, Special Collections Research Center, Syracuse University Libraries; the Newberry Library, Chicago; the Serge Koussevitzky Archive, 1920–76, Music Division, Library of Congress; and Washington National Cathedral, Washington, DC.

Alden, Southworth. Untitled article. *Minneapolis Daily Star*, January 9, 1926.

Ansari, Emily Abrams. *The Sound of a Superpower: Musical Americanism and the Cold War*. Oxford: Oxford University Press, 2018.

Armstrong, Agnes. "American Guild of Organists Centennial: The Examinations and Academic Regalia of the American Guild of Organists." *American Organist* 30, no. 7 (1996): 44–55.

Beckford, Richard. "The Organ Symphony: Its Evolution in France and Transformation in Selected Works by American Composers of the Twentieth Century." DMA diss., Louisiana State University, 1997.

Biggs, E. Power. "Koussevitzky and Concert Hall Organs." *American Organist* 12, no. 3 (March 1978): 28–29.

Borowski, Felix. "Mr. Sowerby's Symphony." *Boston Evening Transcript*, April 13, 1922.

Borowski, Felix. "The Symphony Concert." *Chicago Herald*, February 16, 1918.

Borowski, Felix. "A Young Composer and His Music." *Chicago Herald*, January 19, 1917.

Brown, Rae Linda. *The Heart of a Woman: The Life and Music of Florence B. Price*. Champaign: University of Illinois Press, 2020.

Brune, Adolf. "Mr. Gunn's Orchestral Program of American Music." *Chicago Inter Ocean*, November 19, 1913.

Buckley, Charles. "Hails Creative Genius of Modest Leo Sowerby." *Chicago Herald-American*, November 2, 1952, 4.

Buhrman, T. Scott. "Repertoire and Reviews." *Music: The A.G.O.-R.C.C.O. Magazine* 24 (1941): 102.

Buzard, Stephen. "Leo Sowerby: His Life, Work, and Theology of Church Music." *Journal of the Association of Anglican Musicians* 27 (2018): 1, 4–9.

Buzard, Stephen. "On Big Shoulders: Learning Sowerby at St. James Cathedral, Chicago." *Vox Humana*, October 20, 2017, accessed March 12, 2020, http://www.voxhumana journal.com/buzard2017.html.

C.E.W. "Music in Chicago," *The Music News*, January 1917.

C.E.W. *Music News*, undated article.

Chase, Gilbert. *America's Music*. 2nd rev. ed. New York: McGraw-Hill, 1966.

Cooper, David. *Béla Bartók*. New Haven, CT: Yale University Press, 2015.

Copland, Aaron. "Our Younger Generation—Ten Years Later." *Modern Music* 13, no. 4 (May–June 1936): 3–11.

Cowell, Henry. *American Composers on American Music*. 2nd ed. New York: Frederick Ungar, 1962.

Crociata, Francis. Liner notes to *Corridors of Light: Music of William Ferris*, William Ferris Chorale, William Ferris, conductor. Cedille Records CDR 7004, 2010, compact disc.

Crociata, Francis. Liner notes to *Leo Sowerby: Symphony No. 2, Passacaglia, Interlude & Fugue, Concert Overture, All on a Summer's Day*, Chicago Sinfonietta and Czech National Symphony Orchestra, Paul Freeman, conductor. Cedille Records CDR 90000 039, 1998, compact disc.

Crociata, Francis. Liner notes to *Prairie: Tone Poems by Leo Sowerby*, Czech National Symphony Orchestra, Paul Freeman, conductor. Cedille Records CDR 90000 033, 1997, compact disc.

Dahl, Per. "Text, Identity, and Belief in Stravinsky's Symphony of Psalms." *Danish Musicology Online*, special edition (2016): 61–80.

Dean, Talmage W. *A Survey of Twentieth Century Protestant Church Music in America*. Nashville, TN: Boardman Press, 1988.

Dickinson, Edward. *Music in the History of the Western Church*. New York: Haskell House, 1902.

Donaghey, Frederick. "The Orchestra's Nineteenth." *Chicago Daily Tribune*, February 16, 1918.

Doran, Carol. "Popular Religious Song." In *The Hymnal 1982 Companion*, edited by Raymond F. Glover, 13–28. New York: Church Hymnal Corporation, 1990.

E.B.K. "Gunn Conducts Concert of American Music." *Chicago Tribune*, November 19, 1913, 11.

Ege, Samantha. "Chicago, the 'City We Love to Call Home!': Intersectionality, Narrativity, and Locale in the Music of Florence Beatrice Price and Theodora Sturkow Ryder." *American Music* 39, no. 1 (2021): 1–40.

Ege, Samantha. "Composing a Symphonist: Florence Price and the Hand of Black Women's Fellowship." *Women and Music: A Journal of Gender and Culture* 24 (2020): 7–27.

Epstein, Dena J. "Frederick Stock and American Music." *American Music* 10, no. 1 (1992): 20–52.

Evans, Edwin. "The Salzburg Festival." *Musical Times* 63, no. 955 (1922): 628.

Fansler, Terry. "The Anthem in America: 1900–1950." PhD diss., North Texas State University, 1982.

F.D. "Leo Sowerby's Program." *Chicago Daily Tribune*, January 19, 1917.

Frankenstein, Alfred V. "Twenty-five Years a Conductor." *Review of Reviews* (New York) 81 (January 1930): 96.

French, Florence, ed. "Chicago Composer on Symphony Program." *Musical Leader* 43 (April 13, 1922): 367.

Gann, Kyle. *American Music in the Twentieth Century*. New York: Thomson Wadsworth, 2006.

Gassmann, Remi. "Jubilee Wind-Up." *Modern Music* 18 (1941): 263–64.

Gerlach, Brice. "Leo Sowerby's *The Canticle of the Sun*: An Analysis for Performance." DM diss., Indiana University, 2008.

Ginsburg, Jim. "Francis Crociata / Leo Sowerby: Selected Works for Solo and Duo Piano," Cedille Classical Chicago Podcast, Episode 33. https://www.cedillerecords.org/podcasts/episode-33-francis-crociata-leo-sowerby-selected-works-for-solo-and-duo-piano.

Goss, Madeleine. *Modern Music Makers*. New York: E. P. Dutton, 1952.

Grainger, Percy. "Let Us Sit in Wait No Longer for the Advent of Great American Composers—They Are with Us Already." *Quarter-notes of the Brooklyn Music School Settlement*, December 10, 1919, 1–3.

Grainger, Percy. "My Musical Outlook." In *Grainger on Music*, edited by Malcolm Gillies and Bruce Clunies Ross, 13–28. Oxford: Oxford University Press, 1999.

Grainger, Percy. "The World Music of To-morrow: A Prospect of the Nature of Our Musical Progress Based upon the Musical Tendencies of To-day." *Etude* 34, no. 6 (June 1916): 412.

Groom, Lester W. "Chicago." *American Organist* 11 (1928): 260.

Gunn, Glenn Dillard. "Sowerby Pieces Mystify Hearers at Organ Recital," *Washington Times-Herald*, February 24, 1949.

Gunn, Glenn Dillard. "Sowerby's Recital Reveals New Sacred Music School." *Chicago Herald and Examiner*, undated. Leo Sowerby Papers, Special Collections Research Center, Syracuse University Libraries.

Hackett, Karleton. "Leo Sowerby Reaps Honors in Europe Tour." *Chicago Evening Post*, September 13, 1922.

Hale, Philip. "Sowerby's 'Prairie.'" *Boston Herald*, March 12, 1932.

Halliday, Malcolm. Liner notes for *Impressions: Piano Music of Leo Sowerby*, Malcolm Halliday, piano. Albany Records TR226, 1997, compact disc.

Hanson, Howard. *Music in Contemporary Civilization*. Lincoln: University of Nebraska Press, 1951.

Hanson, Howard. "Report of the Committee on American Music." Music Teachers' National Association, *Proceedings* 33 (1938): 330–34.

Hart, Brian. "Vincent d'Indy and the Development of the French Symphony." *Music & Letters* 87, no. 2 (2016): 237–61.

Henahan, Donal J. "Leo Sowerby, Director, College of Church Musicians." *Cathedral Age* (Fall 1963): 6.

Heyman, Barbara. *Samuel Barber: The Composer and His Music.* 2nd ed. New York: Oxford University Press, 2020.

Hinds, B. Wayne. "Leo Sowerby: A Biography and Descriptive Listing of Anthems." EdD thesis, Georgia Peabody College for Teachers, 1972.

Hitchcock, Wiley. *Music in the United States: A Historical Introduction.* 2nd ed. Englewood Cliffs, NJ. Prentice-Hall, 1974.

Horowitz, Joseph. *Classical Music in America: A History of Its Rise and Fall.* New York: W. W. Norton, 2005.

Howard, John Tasker. *Our Contemporary Composers: American Music in the Twentieth Century.* New York: Thomas Y. Crowell, 1941.

Hubbard, W. L. "America Will Lose Its Greatest Composer If Sowerby Goes Abroad." *Chicago Daily Tribune*, March 6, 1920.

Hume, Paul. "Unrestrained Applause Honors Composer." *Washington Post*, November 19, 1957, B1.

Huntington, Ronald M. Liner notes for *Leo Sowerby: Works for Organ and Orchestra*, David Craighead, David Mulbury, organ, Fairfield Orchestra, John Welsh, conductor. Naxos 8.559028, 1999, compact disc.

Huntington, Ronald M. "A Study of the Musical Contributions of Leo Sowerby." MM thesis, University of Southern California, 1957.

Huntington, Ronald M., ed. *Psalm Oratorio* by Leo Sowerby. Chicago: Leo Sowerby Foundation, 1993.

Jones, Raymond Durward. "Leo Sowerby: His Life and His Choral Music." PhD diss., University of Iowa, 1973.

Kierman, Marilois. "The Compositions of Leo Sowerby for Organ Solo." MM thesis, American University, 1966.

Kirby, Sarah. "Cosmopolitanism and Race in Percy Grainger's American 'Delius Campaign.'" *Current Musicology* 101 (Fall 2017): 39.

Lang, Paul Henry. "Editorial." *Musical Quarterly* 31 (1945): 517.

"Leo Sowerby: A Symposium of Tribute." *Music: The A.G.O.-R.C.C.O. Magazine* 51 (October 1968): 26–27, 64.

Lester, William. "New Music." *The Diapason* 23 (October 1932): 15.

Levy, Beth. *Frontier Figures: American Music and the Mythology of the American West.* Berkeley: University of California Press, 2012.

Martin, Warren. "Three American Composers: Clokey, Sowerby, Lockwood," *Repertoire* 1, no. 2 (November 1951): 114–15.

McLeod, Margie A. "Apathy Drawing Us Back under Foreign Domination, Says Sowerby." *Musical America*, February 12, 1921, 15.

Milligan, Harold. "New Music." *The Diapason* 11 (1920): 21.

Mitchell, Margaret. "Leo Sowerby's Solo Organ Compositions Based on Hymn Tunes." MM thesis, North Texas State University, 1966.

Moore, Edward C. "Noted Cellist Is Heard with the Orchestra." *Chicago Journal*, February 16, 1918.

Morrow, H. L. "Leo Sowerby and His Work for American Church Music." *Musical Times* 73, no. 1074 (1932): 734.

Mowrer, Edgar Ansel. "Americans in Rome Fellows in Academy; Leo Sowerby a Central Figure in Music; His Compatriots Win Honors." *Chicago Daily News*, February 3, 1923.

Ogasapian, John. *Church Music in America, 1620–2000*. Macon, GA: Mercer University Press, 2007.

Oja, Carol. "Forging an International Alliance: Leo Sowerby, Elizabeth Sprague Coolidge, and the Impact of a Rome Prize." In *Music and Musical Composition at the American Academy in Rome*, edited by Martin Brody, 195–21. Rochester, NY: University of Rochester Press, 2014.

Oja, Carol. *Making Music Modern: New York in the 1920s*. New York: Oxford University Press, 2000.

Olmstead, Andrea. "The Rome Prize from Leo Sowerby to David Diamond." In *Music and Musical Composition at the American Academy in Rome*, edited by Martin Brody, 13–41. Rochester, NY: University of Rochester Press, 2014.

Owen, Barbara. *E. Power Biggs, Concert Organist*. Bloomington: Indiana University Press, 1987.

Page, Tim. *Virgil Thomson: Music Chronicles 1940–54*. New York: Library of America, 2014.

Parker, Henry Taylor. Untitled article. *Boston Evening Transcript*, March 12, 1932.

Parks, O. G. "A Critical Analysis of the Works of Leo Sowerby." MM thesis, North Texas State Teachers College, 1941.

Parris, Robert. "A Performer's Companion to Leo Sowerby's *Symphony in G Major* for Organ." DMA diss., Eastman School of Music, 1982.

Phillips, Neill. "A Proposed College of Church Musicians," *Cathedral Age* (Fall 1961): 38–39.

Pollack, Howard. *John Alden Carpenter*. Champaign: University of Illinois Press, 1995.

"Portrait of a Great Man—Leo Sowerby." *Showcase, Music Clubs Magazine* 40, no. 1 (September–October 1960): 10.

Quint, Charles. "Stock Introduces New Sowerby Work." *Musical America*, March 25, 1941, 22.

Quitzow, Charles A. "Sowerby Agitates San Franciscans." *Musical America*, December 2, 1922.

Rayfield, Robert. "A Formal Analysis of the Solo Organ Works of Leo Sowerby to 1960." DM diss., Northwestern University, 1962.

Rayfield, Robert. "Leo Sowerby." *Music: The A.G.O. and R.C.C.O Magazine* 10, no. 11 (1976): 40–41.

Rayfield, Robert. Liner notes to *Sowerby at Trinity*, Faythe Freese, organ. Albany Records Troy 368, 2000, compact disc.

Read-Gehrenbeck, Sarah. "'Why Should the Devil Have All the Pretty Tunes?' The Great Awakening of a New American Idiom: Organ Music Based on Shape-Note Hymns." DM diss., Indiana University, 2017.

"The Report of a Colloquium on the Training of Church Musicians." *Cathedral Age* (Summer 1953): 12–13.

Rich, Alan. "Our Changing Music." *New York Herald Tribune*, October 2, 1963, 19.

Rieke, Edwin. "The Organ Choral Preludes of Leo Sowerby." DMA diss., Eastman School of Music, 1975.

Rorem, Ned. *Knowing When to Stop*. New York: Simon and Schuster, 1994.

Rosenfeld, Maurice. "'All American' Is Concert at Orchestra Hall." *Chicago Examiner*, November 19, 1913, 8.

Rosenfeld, Maurice. "American Concert Is a Big Success," *Musical America*, March 1915.

Rosenfeld, Maurice. "Chicago Concerts of Notable Worth." *Musical America*, January 27, 1917, 42.

Rosenfeld, Maurice. "First Grand Prize in Music to Sowerby; Judges in *The Daily News* Contest Unanimous in Choosing Chicagoan's Work." *Chicago Daily News*, January 28, 1924.

Rosenfeld, Paul. "Musical Chronicle." *The Dial*, December 1924, 532.

Routley, Erik. *Twentieth-Century Church Music*. Rev. ed. London: Herbert Jenkins, 1966.

Sandburg, Carl. *The American Songbag*. New York: Harcourt, Brace, 1927.

Sargent, Joseph. "Forgetting and Remembering: The Case of Leo Sowerby's 'The Canticle of the Sun.'" *American Music* 38, no. 4 (Winter 2020): 485–517.

Sayre, Francis B. Jr. "Sermon, Preached at the Memorial Service for Leo Sowerby Held at St. Thomas Church, New York City, October 27, 1968." *Journal of Church Music* 11 (June 1969): 6.

Schreiber, Lawrence P. "Leo Sowerby." *Music Journal Anthology* (Annual, 1967), 1–2.

Schultz, Rima Lunin. *The Church and the City: A Social History of 150 Years at Saint James, Chicago*. Chicago: Cathedral of Saint James, 1986.

Sears, Lawrence. "Leo Sowerby Had a Varied and Interesting Career." *Washington Evening Star*, October 12, 1968.

Shadle, Douglas. *Antonín Dvořák's New World Symphony*. Oxford: Oxford University Press, 2021.

Shadle, Douglas. *Orchestrating the Nation: The Nineteenth-Century American Symphonic Enterprise*. Oxford: Oxford University Press, 2016.

Sharp, Timothy W. "The Choral Music of Leo Sowerby: A Centennial Perspective." *Choral Journal* 35, no. 8 (1995): 9–15.

Smith, Cecil. "Sowerby's New Work Will Be Given Premiere." *Chicago Daily Tribune*, March 2?, 1941.

Sowerby, Leo. "Church Musician Duties Defined in CCO Lecture." *The Diapason* 50, no. 1 (1958): 8, 40–41.

Sowerby, Leo. "The Compleat Choirmaster." Unpublished manuscript, 1961. The Leo Sowerby Papers, Special Collections Research Center, Syracuse University Libraries.

Sowerby, Leo. "Composition in Relation to the Church and Allied Fields in America." In *Organ and Choral Aspects and Prospects*, edited by Max Hinrichsen, 33–46. London: Hinrichsen Edition, 1958.

Sowerby, Leo. "The Folk-Element—The Vitalizer of Modern Music." *Musical Scrap Book Magazine* 1, no. 1 (1927): 1–2, 11.

Sowerby, Leo. "A Good Creed," *American Organist* 12 (1929): 223.

Sowerby, Leo. *Ideals in Church Music: An Official Statement Prepared for the Joint Commission on Church Music of the Protestant Episcopal Church in the United States of America*. Greenwich, CT: Seabury Press, 1956.

Sowerby, Leo. "Leading Composer Writes of Changed Standards." *The Diapason* 51 (1959): 45.

Sowerby, Leo. Letter to the *Chicago Music News*, January 6, 1915.

Sowerby, Leo. "Music at St. James'." *Diocese of Chicago* 10 (October 1934): 39.

Stallings, V. Lee. "A Study of *Forsaken of Man*, a Sacred Cantata by Leo Sowerby." MSM thesis, Southern Baptist Theological Seminary, 1956.

Stolter, Mark Evan. "The Influence of the American Orchestral Organ on Selected Works of Leo Sowerby." DMA diss., University of Kansas, 2019.

Stover, Harold. "Leo Sowerby at 100." *New England Organist* 5, no. 3 (May–June 1995), https://www.albany.edu/piporg-l/Sowerby.html.

Stubbs, G. Edward. "Ecclesiastical Music." *New Music Review and Church Music Review* 21, no. 241 (December 1921): 417.

Taruskin, Richard. *Stravinsky and the Russian Traditions: A Biography of the Works through Mavra*. Oxford: Oxford University Press, 1996.

Tawa, Nicholas. *The Great American Symphony: Music, the Depression, and War*. Bloomington and Indianapolis: Indiana University Press, 2009.

Thompson, Randall. "The Contemporary Scene in American Music." *Musical America*, April 25, 1932, 9–17.

Tischler, Barbara L. *An American Music: The Search for an American Musical Identity*. New York and Oxford: Oxford University Press, 1986.

Tuthill, Burnet C. "Leo Sowerby." *Musical Quarterly* 24 (1938): 249–64.

Von Glahn, Denise. *The Sounds of Place: Music and the American Cultural Landscape*. Boston: Northeastern University Press, 2003.

Von Rhein, John. "Belated Amends." *Chicago Tribune*, May 4, 1990, https://www.chicago tribune.com/news/ct-xpm-1990-05-04-9002060742-story.html.

Walsh, Stephen. "Stravinsky's Choral Music." *Tempo* 81 (1967): 44–45.

Webb, Lucile Hammill. "A Study of the G Major Symphony for Organ by Leo Sowerby." MM thesis, Eastman School of Music, 1945.

Weber, Henriette. "Sowerby in Fourfold Success." *Chicago Examiner*, February 16, 1918.

Williams, David McK. "The Modernist in Church Music." New York: Hymn Society, 1935.

Wright, Farnsworth. "One Great Composer Our Need in America, Urges DeLamarter." *Musical America*, February 3, 1917, 35.

Wright, Searle. "Seth Daniels Bingham: 100th Anniversary." *American Organist* 16, no. 6 (June 1982): 40–44.

Wyton, Alec. "Twentieth Century American Church Music." In *Duty and Delight: Routley Remembered: A Memorial Tribute to Erik Routley (1917–1982)*, edited by Robin A. Leaver, James H. Litton, and Carlton R. Young, 79–88. Carol Stream, IL: Hope Publishing Company, 1985.

Zak, Rose A. "Dialogue and Discourse in Stravinsky's 'Symphony of Psalms.'" *Criticism* 22, no. 4 (Fall 1980): 357–75.

# INDEX

**JOSEPH SARGENT** is an assistant professor of musicology at the University of Alabama.

The University of Illinois Press
is a founding member of the
Association of University Presses.

___________________________

University of Illinois Press
1325 South Oak Street
Champaign, IL 61820-6903
www.press.uillinois.edu